Bipolar
Barbie

K Y L E   B I S H O P

Order this book online at www.trafford.com
or email orders@trafford.com

Most Trafford titles are also available at major online book retailers.

Printed in the United States of America.

ISBN: 978-1-4269-7450-2 (sc)
ISBN: 978-1-4269-7451-9 (e)

Trafford rev. 07/31/2012

   www.trafford.com

North America & international
toll-free: 1 888 232 4444 (USA & Canada)
phone: 250 383 6864 ♦ fax: 812 355 4082

Preface

THE NEEDLE WENT in and I felt nothing. He was good because he had been doing this all his life. He was twelve years old when he started using a needle. The meth washed over me. I had never felt this way before, it was too much. I knew then, in that moment, that he didn't care or love me anymore. I had seen what happened to the girls who were hooked on meth by these men and then left with an addiction. That was not the place I wanted to be, being passed around like a meth whore looking for the next shot. I knew I had to leave, and quickly. I slipped into sweat pants, his old t-shirt, old running shoes and a jacket. I ran for the door and across the yard to the neighbors. I told them to call the police to pick me up, they were cooking meth and I had to get out. I ran through the yards until I came to a fence and had to get in the lake. I kept running until I got to the bridge where I had asked the neighbors to tell the police to pick me up. I hid in the growth by the lake crouched down. My mouth was dry, my hands were sweating and I was breathing very hard. I heard him calling my name. He was looking for me. Right then the police car pulled up and I jumped in and laid down in the backseat so no one would see me.

Chapter 1

MY MOTHER HAD me when she was sixteen. It says eighteen on my birth certificate but she verified she was actually sixteen. I had done the math. I knew she was sixteen. She told me she had me so she would have someone to love her unconditionally. From the way she has treated me, I have to say her actions speaks louder than words. Maybe a dog would have loved her unconditionally with that kind of treatment. The dog might have loved her but I don't know what kind of life or how long of a life that dog would have. After all, she had Coco put to sleep.

I'm starting with my childhood because I think it had a profound effect on me. My mother was an alcoholic. It explains a lot of what my mother did to me. My nerves were shot before I got to the third grade. I was also depressed as a child. Things were always out of balance at my house. I wonder if this had anything to do with my being Bipolar. I really don't know.

I was around two in my first memory. I still remember, because it was traumatizing. A lady from the apartment building we lived in coming to get me and take me to swing. My mother was screaming so loud and for so long a woman came to my rescue. She knocked on the door and my mother handed me to her. I remember swinging. I don't remember her taking me back to my mother.

I remember when we moved once. My mother screamed at me unmercifully. I remember two men. One of them gave me a miniature camera. I went into another room and looked at the camera. I don't remember anything else. I remember my mother and daddy spelling watermelon in front of me and I said watermelon. I remember the looks on their faces. I don't remember the watermelon.

My cousin and I ate all the icing off my birthday cake. We were at my paternal grandparents' home and we had a pretty big family. When someone came looking for us we were on top of a counter eating the icing off the cake. The cake had no icing on it when whoever found us. I don't remember anything else. One of my cousins had a birthday party on the Bozo Show. I remember being chosen to pass out the cookies that day. I remember pieces of the ride to the television studio. I don't remember anything else about that day.

My next memory was of being hit by a mail truck. In those days mail trucks were big and made of steel. I was four. I was crossing the street to get the mail from the mailman. This day he didn't stop at our mail box. This day the mail truck hit me. I felt the hit on my right side. I was blacked out. I remember coming in the yard with my mother sitting about a foot away from me, not too close, not touching me. I can still see her face. She didn't notice I had come until I sat up and asked her "What happened?" She told me I had been hit by the mail truck. I can still see her face, blank and cold. I'm still wondering why it didn't hurt. I remember the impact of the truck hitting my right hip and then I blacked out. My Daddy was down the street screaming at the mail man. The mail man told my Daddy that he was just back to work after hitting and killing another kid. I guess my Daddy felt sorry for the "child killing mailman". Nothing was ever done. I wasn't even taken to the hospital. Life went on and I don't remember anything else. My right side has always hurt more than my left side.

Getting on her nerves got me to a private school for the first grade. It also got my Daddy working three jobs to pay for the school. The first day all the children were crying for their mothers. This was confusing to me. I asked the teacher why they were crying and told her I wanted to learn to read. That year was a roller coaster. I don't remember what I ate for lunch. Everyone had to bring a lunch prepared by their mother. I don't remember a single thing I ate at school. I'm sure it wasn't special or I would have remembered. I remember the boy with the glass eye. He would take it out and show it to people. I didn't want to see. I paid attention and soon I could read.

I was four when I enrolled in a private first grade class. The teacher's name was Ms. White. The classroom was in the basement at her house. My mother didn't want me disturbing her anymore so that was to my advantage. My birthday is in October and I would have had to wait another year to go to school. My mother was tired of reading to me. We went to the library at least once a week. I loved Dr. Sue books. I had to beg, plead, and beg some more to get her to quit reading her book and read to me instead.

Ms. White would ask my mother if I could go to the mall with her after school or run errands. She did this frequently. She took me home. I think she felt sorry for me. She was always sweet and the only thing I remember doing was going to a store and buying a vase. I know she took me home many other days but I don't remember what we did on those days. I'm sure if there had been Children's Protective Services they would have been called.

When the year was over I took the test to pass the first grade. I remember going to downtown Birmingham and someone breaking a large plate glass window. This was 1962 or 1963 and race relations were a big issue. My mother told me not to look and to keep walking. I took the test, passed, and went to the public school for the second grade.

I loved music. I remember shocking myself with the record player plug when I was trying to plug it in to listen to Elvis' song, "Little Sister". When I put the plug in the socket my finger was on one of the prongs. This record was one of the smallest records with one song on each side. I don't remember any other records so I listened to the Elvis records that belonged mostly to my mother. I would shut the door to my room and play that record over and over. After I got shocked I didn't try to plug in the record player again. I remember my mother's reaction to me, her anger was shocking. I couldn't ask her to plug in the record player so I don't remember listening to music anymore, not unless I was in the car.

The day when Coco was taken to the vet, we were on our way to the mall to get our picture taken with Santa Claus. I was thinking and I asked when Coco was coming home. My brother was in the backseat with me. My mother told us then, in the car, that Coco had been put to sleep. We didn't know what that was so I asked her again when the dog was coming home. She said never, that Coco had been put to sleep. I don't remember any picture with Santa Claus so I don't know if we made one or not.

In that era people smoked in the car without cracking the windows or anything. So riding in the car wasn't my favorite place either after that drive.

Chapter 2

THE SECOND GRADE was eventful. I loved school. I played school when I wasn't at school. People at school didn't scream or be mean. Then I had a new baby sister. I already had a brother. I remember I was wearing white boots and the teacher had just told me to stand still in line. Just as she had told me to be still my Daddy was there. He told me I had a sister. I wasn't excited. That just meant my mother would have more reasons to scream and no time for me or my brother. My brother and I was bed wetter. We slept in the same bed since his bedroom had been taken over by our new baby sister. My mother would put us to bed by hollering "It's time to go to bed. Get in there and go to sleep." The sheets were still wet from the night before. I don't know how my brother coped. I taught myself how to go to sleep in the stinky bed. I lay on my hands to make myself be still and trained myself to go to sleep. I let myself go and not think about anything and the next thing I knew it was morning. The bed was freshly wet and my mother was screaming.

I was awakened by my mother's scream, "You're going to be late to school. Get up now." I got up, found some clothes to put on, and ran out the door. I walked to school. It wasn't very far but I had to run and I was late more times than not. I had no friends, no one to eat lunch with. I was the last one picked to play any game we were playing. My school years were sad and I was nervous. My hands and feet sweated so much that my papers would be soaked when I finished. I was a nervous wreck.

The race relations were in full swing. I had a fourth grade teacher that was colored. She was the only colored person I had seen up close. She lived to torture me. I was at an awkward stage. My clothing and grooming situation told her she could torment me and get away with doing so. I had three outfits given to me by the girl next door. This teacher lived to torment me. I walked home every day and told my mother through all the tears and sobbing what this teacher was doing to me. She didn't even call the school. I don't remember her doing anything. She didn't call the principal. She didn't comfort me. She was reading. She didn't have time to do anything else. She was always someplace else in a book.

When I was seven, eight years old my mother did buy a contraption that was like a window screen I slept on. She did cover it with a sheet. It had an alarm and it sensed wetness. After about two months I wasn't a bed wetter anymore.

I started the ninth grade in my high school. I didn't wet the bed anymore. I made a few friends. My mother bought me clothes. For the first time in my life I actually had clothes. Of course my mother thought we could share clothes. She had body odor under her arms that was so bad I told her she couldn't wear my clothes. Her clothes stunk so bad I didn't want to wear her stinky clothes. I don't know why she couldn't smell the funk on them. It wasn't contained to under the arms. All you had to do was open the closet door. After I told her that she wasn't so interested in buying my clothes. I had a few outfits but I had to wear the same clothes week after week. This is one time I told the truth about what I wanted and didn't want. I usually told people what I thought they wanted to hear so they wouldn't get mad at me and like me.

High School wasn't bad. I was allowed to date from the time I was thirteen. I asked my mother when I was about ten years old if anyone would ever want to marry me. We had just gotten back from my Daddy's bosses house and his daughter had moved back home. She was getting her third divorce. I asked my mother if anyone would ever want to marry me. She said "If that girl can get married three times I'm sure you will find someone that will want to marry you." That answer went straight to my heart, the very soul of me. I've never forgotten those words or the tone of voice she used. It is still stuck in my mind. Those few words affected my life in a big way.

There was a lot of stress in my house. My daddy worked nights but he was awake a lot of the time when I got home. My mother went to work. I took care of the house cleaning and I cooked dinner. I was twelve. If I came in and my Daddy was hollering and screaming I knew the electric bill had come. He slammed the kitchen doors and hollered. I tip toed around. When he finished his episode I cleaned and cooked. My mother came in from work and dinner was ready. I ate very little because my Daddy would eat what I didn't eat so I saved some for him because I knew he was still hungry.

The biggest thing that happened in the fourth grade was a girl actually wanted to be my friend. I spent the night at her house. Her mother didn't like her being away from home so we always spent the night at her house. I was glad about that.

About this time my cousin was coming over to spend the night. I was eleven because we talked about bras in the bathtub. I thought we had privacy because the door was shut. I guess my mother heard because for Christmas I got a training bra. My mother then proceeded to tell everyone that I was now wearing a bra. That year we went to her brother's house and my aunt asked me about the bra. I think that should have been one of those mother daughter things. I was embarrassed that she told everyone and they laughed at me. I felt so small.

During that bath my cousin wanted to wash me and I wash her. I didn't like the sound of that so we got out of the bath tub. I felt funny about what had occurred in the bathtub but I didn't tell anyone. She was my cousin and we had a good time together. We didn't take anymore baths together.

I would often feel like I was smaller than my body. I felt like I was small but I was inside a body that was big. I've never told anyone this because I don't know how to explain the feeling that I had every night at bedtime. I always cried myself to sleep. I was so miserable. I was afraid I was going to die and I had no one that I could talk about this feeling. I remember my Daddy coming home from work on Saturday mornings and making my brother in letting me watch the cartoons that I'd liked, The Jetson's and the Flintstones. He would flip a coin. He would tell my brother, "if heads then she wins, if tails you lose". At the time I didn't catch on either but later I figured it out and it is one great memory I have during my childhood. I knew where I stood with my mother. She treated me with a cold, uninterested, disregard. I wasn't important to her. I didn't see anything that she did that was loving.

Chapter 3

I LOVED GOING to church. I don't know what I wore but I dressed myself and proceeded to obtain transportation to Sunday school, Church, Bible Training, Choir, and Wednesday night services and Choir practice. My Daddy drove me nine times out of ten. My parents had taken me one Sunday and I liked it there. My Sunday school teacher was nice I guess. I don't remember much that I did but I was there. I remember looking up verses in Bible Classes because I always tried to be first to find the scripture.

I went to a huge church. I know I was little and anything could have seemed big, but I knew it was big because there was a balcony for people. The first time, my parents took me and they had the Lord's Supper. I took the wafer and I took the juice in the little glass. I liked the little glass so I took it home with me. When I showed my Daddy he told me I was stealing. I thought they were free to take home. We went to the night service that day and I returned the little glass. I had to apologize for taking the glass. I have shop lifted a couple of times, but the Church incident is always on my mind.

Remember I am Bipolar and I don't know when it started, if you are born with this disease, or how it begins. I suppose these are questions for my Psychiatrist. I've just never asked. I haven't studied up on Bipolar disorder. This is how my life went until I was diagnosed seven years ago. Until now I've been embarrassed to tell people and I just haven't given the technicalities. These things are what happened to me. Your disease may be radically different. Either way Bipolar is Bipolar. The looks and the shock will still be there. It's this attitude about this disease is how people look at bipolar. Together we can take away the stigma. We can take away the shame. We can gain a place in this world that accepts Bipolar as a disease like any other disease. How the disease presents in each of us may be different but together we can take away the shame and stigma attached to Bipolar. Even on our bad days we should be treated with dignity and respect.

Chapter 3

M Y DADDY HAD bought me a 1965 Mustang when I turned fifteen before I met the boy that was to be my first husband. For months I had been looking in the Sunday paper for cars. I didn't think I would actually get a car until my Daddy started looking at the paper. We started taking test drives. My Daddy had found a teal Mustang with white interior and it was a convertible. We were on the road that goes around the airport. My Daddy was driving slowly, showing me how the gears worked and what the motor would sound like when I needed to change gears. All of a sudden there was a huge bump that knocked us up the road. I asked my Daddy if the car had blown up. He said "No, this woman just hit us." That was a totaled car. The lady had insurance that paid for the car.

The search was still on. The next car was a 65 Mustang also.

It was in great condition on the inside. It has black interior which was still in perfect condition. It was jacked up, an unusual shade of green with a Hurst shifter. I was fifteen and had my own car. Next was learning how to drive a three speed. My Daddy insisted on me learning to drive a manual transmission so I could drive anything.

I was almost sixteen when I learned to drive with the clutch and shifter. We went for driving lessons as often as we could for as long as both of our nerves could take. The first time I drove the car out of the driveway and on the road I had a miracle parking occurrence. The neighborhood we lived in was on a hill with a lot of ups and downs and curves. I had just started out of the subdivision, about three minutes after I left the driveway. A car was coming and there were cars parked on both sides of the road so there wasn't room for both of us to go through. This car just came up a hill so I didn't have much time to get out of the way. Daddy said pull in over here. There were two cars on that side of the road. Essentially I needed to Park. I froze up, Daddy's hollering wasn't helping but he was scared we were going to have a calamity for sure. My brother was in the back and a friend of his. I closed my eyes because I just froze up. When I opened my eyes my car was perfectly between the two cars on the street. Daddy asked me how I got the car where it was sitting. I told him "I don't know. I closed my eyes." There was some hollering about never closing my eyes when I drive. I consider the incident a miracle. God had to have parked that car where it was. That's the only explanation I have for not having a head on collision less than a mile from my home.

I know it was God because I have always been protected by God. I've been in too many situations that I should have died and by some miracle I didn't. I was baptized on my twelfth birthday. I was reborn on my twelfth birthday and to me that was a miracle that my baptism happened on my birthday. I had been going to Huffman Baptist Church since I could remember as a young girl. I was moved by the Holy Spirit during the worship service that morning. My Daddy was outside waiting to pick me up. I was taking so long because there were prayers and talking to the Pastor. It took about thirty minutes after the Service. My Daddy came looking for me. When he saw what I was doing, he cried. I cried. He cried for a little bit. Just some tears, no sobbing or such, just a few tears.

Chapter 4

M Y COUSIN AND I were close. She lived across town in
Bessemer, Alabama but we managed to get together every
weekend. My mother would let us take her car. My cousin was a year
older than me and had her driver's license. We would drive to the mall.
After the mall closed all the teenagers rode around the mall. If you saw
a guy you liked you would honk at him. If he liked the way you looked
he would tell you to pull over. We did one particular night. This guy had
longish blonde hair and had with him his Chevrolet Camaro. We talked
for a little while. I gave him my phone number. He called me and I went
on our first date. I don't remember where we went. We dated for about
six months and we were going steady. I was fifteen.

I drank my first beer and smoked my first marijuana with him. I didn't
like the smell of the marijuana or what it did to me but I smoked anyway.
Everyone else was and they liked it a lot. They were older than me. I was
fifteen and my boyfriend was 20. These people were his friends.

I lost my virginity to him. I was scared but it wasn't too awful.

We were in the den downstairs and my parents were upstairs asleep with
the fan on. I always came home at the time they told me.

The whole act took about 3 minutes and I didn't understand the big
deal. The next time we tried to have sex he had too much to drink and

couldn't get an erection. I didn't know anything about this but he had me worked into frenzy. I drank a little beer myself. I had no inhibitions. I guess technically he took my virginity with a bottle. I didn't know what he was doing. I had my eyes closed and I was still wondering what the big deal was. He broke my hymen with that bottle and blood was everywhere when he got up. It just occurred to me as I'm writing this that he was so small in the penis department he couldn't break my hymen with his penis. I didn't know it was a bottle until after it was over. I was shocked. I was dumbfounded. I was freaked out and I felt violated.

I saw all the blood and immediately jumped up. I knew he had broken my hymen. I knew I had to wash all my sheets and bedding. The washer and dryer were downstairs across from the den in the garage. It was about one o'clock in the morning so I put all the bloody bedding in the washer. I prayed no one wouldn't wake up and find out what I was doing. I remembered what my Daddy had told me and I remembered what my mother had told me. My Daddy told me "You don't buy the cow if you can get the milk for free." My mother told me basically that if someone wanted to get married to me I might not get a second chance when she said what she did about Mr. Austin's daughter. She was referring to the one that had been married three times. This was my chance to marry I thought. I actually thought it might be my one and only chance.

It was settled. I had to marry him. My self-esteem was so low. No one ever told me I was pretty. No one told me how special I was. We got engaged and he bought me a tiny diamond ring with silver around it to make it look bigger.

My cousin and I shopped for my dress. My mother wasn't interested in doing this with me. She wanted to divorce my Daddy and date so she wanted me to get married at sixteen. She later confessed to me over the phone and she was drunk. She is a lovely woman. I am a sarcastic person, she was the worst mother a girl could have with the exception of really horrible mothers that allow molestation and rape go on without doing anything. I was blessed that I didn't have that to contend with. I just had to contend with having a great big heart, wearing my feelings on my sleeve and a mother that was miserable.

My cousin and I went downtown and looked in all the stores for my wedding dress. I didn't know this was something a mother and daughter usually did together. I found a white wedding dress I wanted and I called my mother. She told me I could buy the dress. I don't know much about the wedding plans. I was fifteen.

The wedding was to take place at the church we were members of two weeks after I turned sixteen. My daddy offered me a new car and modeling lessons if I wouldn't get married. As we were outside the church he told me I didn't have to do this. We could leave right now. My mother's words still hung in my mind and I thought I would never have a chance to get married if I didn't go through with this wedding. I thought the ceremony would change me. I thought the ceremony would make me feel different. It didn't. I walked down the aisle to a boy in a leisure suit dressed in a white wedding dressed. I was embarrassed by what he was wearing but I had to go through with the ceremony. I was sure something special would happen to us. I was sure everything would change.

We went to my parents' house for the reception. There was cake. I don't remember anything else about the reception. I went downstairs to my bedroom, changed my clothes and he and I left for our honeymoon. One night in a motel, we were late so all they had to eat was spaghetti. We had left the reception without telling anyone. When we got to our room I called my daddy. I told him I loved him. The wedding night was very disappointing. Nothing had changed. I was sixteen and married. I had a mustang.

We left the motel about eleven am and went to my parents' house where we would live until the trailer my uncle gave me was ready to live in. It had to be cleaned, etc.

We lived with my parents for about three weeks I guess. One Sunday afternoon we came out of my room and I had some stuff packed and we told him we were going to live in the trailer. We didn't have any furniture. My daddy got a loan for us and we bought some cheap furniture that was horrendous but he wanted to have walking around money. I think he spent it on pot, I don't know.

He made one hundred dollars a week. I soon found out that paying bills and buying groceries wasn't possible with that hundred dollars. I didn't buy many groceries. I don't remember what I ate.

It became winter. I had registered in the High School for the area we lived in. The first day of school I found out I was pretty and plenty of boys would be interested in me. They were carrying on and the teacher said "She's married." That ended that. I was married and there were boys in that high school my age that thought I was pretty. They were talking about me in a good way. I never thought I was pretty. My teeth were horrible. My permanent teeth came in. My two front teeth were so far apart it was ugly, my eye tooth on the left side never came in and the right eye tooth was just a stub. I begged for braces until I got them. I ended up wearing braces five years and still ended up with teeth that were ugly.

I couldn't get out of bed because it was so cold. The heat in the trailer didn't work. I had to stay in bed to be warm. I had a space heater next to the bed and I slept all the time. When I returned to school they told me I had missed so many days I might as well get a GED.

Instead I got a job at Liberty National Life Insurance Company in downtown Birmingham. I was sixteen. I told them I was eighteen and had graduated from high school. They gave me a test, I passed and I was hired to be a file clerk. I recognized my boss. He was the father of a girl I went to high school with and I was surprised he didn't recognize me. While I worked at Liberty National I decided being married was for the birds. My parents had moved to Texas. My mother had hounded my Daddy to get another job so he would make more money. He did make more money.

I got a divorce. I couldn't take being married and broke anymore. He told me he hadn't wanted to marry me in the first place.

Chapter 5

I WAS STAYING with my cousin. She was dating a guy who had a friend. The friend was sort of good looking and he was wild about me. He had a Trans Am like in Smokey and the Bandit. We started dating. Then he told me he loved me and I guess I told him I loved him. I hadn't taken any time to think about what I was doing. I was just doing. It was about three months before he made love to me. That was actually the first time I had been made love to. He was wonderful to me. He took me out, he fed me. He let me drive his car. He was so wonderful. We dated about a year and he proposed to me. He had a ring and everything.

It was time for school to start and I left my cousins and went to Texas. All the furniture had been moved by a moving company. My mother didn't tell me to take my jewelry out of my dresser. I had rings that guys had bought me and I wanted to keep them. They were taken. I just didn't know to take them out before my mother took off to Texas. My parents got a three bedroom apartment. It had a pool.

My boyfriend drove my car and my brother to Texas. He was supposed to fly back to Birmingham. I went and registered for High School and was really looking forward to being a teenager. I knew what I did wrong. I knew how to do it right this time. My boyfriend was there for about two days. My mother asked me to go to the grocery store. At the grocery store she told me she wanted to divorce my daddy and we were going back to Birmingham. I wanted to stay with my daddy in Texas but I couldn't find my voice. I was so used to telling people what they wanted to hear, my mother was crying and I was telling her everything would be alright. My boyfriend loved the idea and was so glad he wouldn't be so far from me. He slept outside my cousin and aunts house in the car with me. There wasn't a bed for me so for two nights I slept outside in the car with my boyfriend.

My mother rented an apartment and had all the furniture returned to Birmingham. I lived with my mother and went to work for an alcoholic diabetic attorney. He hired me, gave me a key to his office. I was working the second week and had not seen hide or hair of him. People kept coming in giving me money. I didn't know what it was for; I didn't have a receipt book. I took the money and hid it in the library in a law book. One day late in the second week a woman shows up and asks me if anyone has brought in money. I said yes and went to get it out of the book. I don't even know how much money was there.

The next week the attorney finally showed up. I was glad he didn't do much because I learned to type there. I worked there about a year and a half. I paid for parking. Sometimes my boyfriend would meet me outside after work and drive me the five blocks to where my car was parked. He was so good to me. He spent every night with me. He gave me massages until I wasn't tense anymore and then he made love to me. We had simultaneous orgasms. He was so good to me.

My brother and sister were there. My sister's bedroom was my mother's also. One night my mother didn't come home at all. My sister was scared to death. I started calling hospitals. She walks in about thirty minutes later and tells us she was at the bar all night watching some man do magic. I didn't know enough then to know she was actually sleeping with some man after she got drunk and picked one up. Her whole reason for getting a divorce was so she could date.

She told me some years later, while she was drunk, that she had let me get married at sixteen so she would just have two kids to take care of. She had bullied my daddy into believing if I didn't get married I would elope. My mother is a mess.

My mother decided she had to move to a cheaper apartment.

My boyfriend was still spending every night with me. He was still massaging me until I was limp and making love to me. I learned what an orgasm was when we made love. We had simultaneous orgasms. I always had an orgasm when he made love to me.

One day I come in and my boyfriend wasn't there yet. He lived across town with his grandparents and drove about 28 miles to me everyday, except on the weekends when he stayed all weekend. So my mother tells me he needs to pay rent or we need to get our own place. I told my boyfriend that night that we should get married before I changed my mind. I was seventeen. I didn't tell him my mother wanted him to pay rent. I felt like that was prostituting me out. He was already feeding me every night. He was taking care of me. All we did was make love and sleep in my bedroom. My bedroom was next to hers, her love life was in the toilet, she was drinking like a fish and I guess she heard us and couldn't take my "happiness" anymore.

That's the thing about my mother. Every time she knocked me down I got back up and make lemonade out of lemons. She wasn't right in the head.

We got married two days later at his aunt's house. It was a small ceremony. I wore a blue dress that I had worn about a month prior to his cousin's wedding. My daddy was listening on the phone. He didn't have time to drive down from Arkansas it happened so fast. I guess we had a cake, I don't remember.

We left for our honeymoon. Everyone thought we were going to Florida. We didn't have time for that. We went to a very nice hotel. We got in the room and the lovemaking started. We stayed in that room for three days making love. It was great. I will always remember him. He was so good to me. He took the place of parents I didn't have.

I was still working for the attorney. One day, after I got back from my Grandfather's funeral, he just told me I was fired. I called him and told his wife where I was going and why. I had never called in sick or missed a day of work for that year or longer.

Now I was married to a man that worked for Alabama Power and he made enough money I didn't have to work. I don't remember how I spent my time. I remember paying the car payment once and I remember my Daddy and stepmother coming over for dinner. I don't remember what I cooked.

One year for my birthday he gave me a surprise party. He gift to me was a necklace that had faith, hope, and love charms. I loved it. My mother and my cousin attended also. I don't remember any other presents, I don't remember the cake but I'm sure I had one.

He went back to school at UAB (University of Alabama in Burmingham) for his degree in engineering. My cousin started coming to see me. She wanted us to get an apartment together. I thought that sounded like fun—remember I'm Bi-Polar and had no one to guide me.

Chapter 6

S O I LEFT him and got an apartment in the building my mother lived in. My cousin and I got an apartment. We didn't have any furniture except what was in the bedrooms. I had my mother and Daddy's king size bed somehow and my great grandfathers chest of drawers that had belonged to him when he was a child. I guess it was built sometime in the 1800's.

We went out to bars; neither of us was old enough. She was tall like me with short blonde hair. We were both five feet eight inches tall. I had long black hair. The shoes were worn were platforms with about four inch heels on them so that made us over six feet tall. We got noticed when we walked in the door. We didn't pay any attention and I didn't know men were gaga about long legs. We were just having a good time and didn't take anybody at those bars seriously.

Eventually my cousin got a boyfriend. I was just dating. I didn't have a boyfriend. He was ok. His head was too big but she liked him. We were listening to the Rolling Stones "Some Girls" and her boyfriend had brought a joint over one week night. We smoked the joint and decided that putting detergent in the big fountain in Vestavia was a good idea. We bought the biggest box of detergent they made. We were riding in his orange Camaro. We were still listening to "Some Girls" by the Rolling Stones. We were having a big time. We put the soap in the fountain. We made the mistake of going back and looking at the bubbles. There was a bunch. After we looked we took the same road on our way home. Doing something like that in an orange car is not good. The police pulled us over. We had the box of detergent still in the car. They took all of us and separated us. I don't know who cracked and told them what we had done. No one really needed to tell anyone, we had the box. The police man I talked to was nice. I was crying. He asked me what we were doing and all I could say is "Please don't arrest me, I want to be an Attorney." They let us go and told us it was up to the accountant that owned the fountain. We decided to be at his office first thing in the morning. No one slept. My cousin and I had to call in sick. Her boyfriend owned a brass bed store. I was Executive Assistant to the Regional Manager of Equifax. My cousin was a dental assistant.

When we got there the man wasn't in yet. We waited. About fifteen minutes later he invited us into his office. We talked to him but I don't remember what we said. He made us all pay five dollars to flush out the fountain and told us not to worry about anything. He wasn't going to press any charges. Want to talk about being relieved. The police had told us if the accountant wanted to press charges they would come to our work and arrest us. I knew nothing good could come of that.

My mother still lived upstairs in the apartment building my cousin and I lived in. One morning I answered the phone. It was the place she worked and they said she hadn't come in. They were concerned about her so I went upstairs to see what was going on. I had a key so after I knocked a couple of times before I let myself in. I found her on the bed wearing black with her hands across her chest. There was blood. I knew what she had done. I went down the hall screaming and some friends let me use their phone to call one of my boyfriends that happened to be a Sheriff in Jefferson County. He told me to call 911 and that he was on his way. He got to me before the ambulance got there. He was in uniform so he talked to the ambulance people. She had left a note saying not to call an ambulance, to go to the bank and get the $400 check cashed because

I would need the money. I wasn't working at the time. I guess I got let go from Equifax. I really don't remember. They didn't know if she would live or die for two days. My uncle and aunt came from Georgia. I was glad I wasn't alone. The doctors wanted to see anybody who might know why she would try to kill herself. I had the Sheriff go with me and my uncle accompanied us. We went through a series of locked doors and finally got to the right room. The doctor was sitting there. When he asked why she might try to kill herself my uncle said "She hasn't been the same since Elvis died." I didn't know what to say. I thought I'm glad I've got the law with me because he might get locked up too. It's hilarious now but at the time I was horrified. My uncles a good ole boy but he drinks a lot.

I got home and called my Daddy. My mother was the only reason I was still in Birmingham. I asked my Daddy if I could come and live with him if she died. He was in Arkansas. He had remarried six weeks after the divorce was final. He did call my mother and tell her if she wasn't coming back he was getting married the next day. He's been married to that woman for a long, long time. He said he didn't have room for me. I was still 17. I told him I would never tell him I didn't have room for him if I lived in one room. I guess I hung the phone up. It was too much for me. I don't know how I dealt with this.

Unfortunately, my mother lived. I went and bought her night gowns. I didn't know what she needed. I visited during visiting hours. Two weeks later they let her out. My face broke out in huge bumps. I have never had complexion problems. I went to the dermatologist. I don't know what he did but eventually the bumps went away. They left scars on my checks. I use a prescription product to keep them from showing.

My mother got another job somewhere and she waitressed at a bar in Bessemer. She moved to Georgia shortly thereafter. My uncle came and got her. She left me in Birmingham. I was all alone and had no one or nothing.

After all that I was working at the car dealership. I loved my job and my boss. My cousin got mad at me and moved out with her boyfriend and didn't tell me anything. She had the phone transferred. It was in her name. I had to pay all the bills. I couldn't afford a telephone. Everyone had left me all alone. Sometime in all this mess I turned 18. At this time I worked at a car dealership in the office. I didn't make enough money to buy food so when I got paid I bought a bag of potatoes and ate potatoes every night for about seven months. My mother got me a gig slinging drinks at the bar where she worked. I didn't like doing this but the tips were nice. I did this for about three weeks.

One day my boss at the car dealership told me he knew about me working at Sonny's bar. He told me to quit and he gave me a raise. I quit. I still had to eat potatoes. On Fridays he would give me $20 out of petty cash. He said I didn't have to repay the money. I guess he knew I wasn't eating lunch or drinking soda. I didn't have any money.

Chapter 7

WHILE I WAS at the bar my mother decided the bouncer was a good looking man. She said I should talk to him. I did and he started coming over to my house. We were dating. His mother had tried to kill herself so he knew how I felt I guess. His mother had tried to kill herself also. I didn't think I deserved any better and I needed someone. He only had the bouncer job. Somehow we decided to get married. I was tired of being alone. He got a job as a machinist and started the Monday after we got married on Friday night at the preacher's house. This time I wore a peach dress that wasn't long. I bought it that day. I also bought the rings.

My daddy, my stepmother, my brother and my sister and my mother were there. It was a short ceremony. No cake, no reception, no honeymoon. My daddy did take us out to eat. I was embarrassed. We went back to the apartment that had no TV or telephone. We got in bed and he went to sleep. I went to sleep. I didn't know what I was doing. I needed someone who cared about me so bad. I needed guidance and I had no one. The next day we went antiquing with my daddy and stepmother. I saw all kinds of beautiful things that at the time I had no hope of ever having. I still had my great grandfather's chest. I loved that chest. When we got done antiquing we went back to the apartment and sat there.

We didn't make love, we didn't have sex. We were just there. I wasn't in love with him. I married him because I didn't think I deserved any one better. How much self esteem can you have when your mother tries to kill herself and your daddy doesn't have room for you? How much self esteem can you have when you've never been told you were beautiful?

Evan and I moved out of the apartment and into a trailer on the lake. I had to give my mother my car because I couldn't pay the payments and she got it sold. Later I found out I should have gone to my grandfather, Poppy, he would have paid for it so I could keep it. Oh well. I still don't know what I was thinking. We rode to work together. I dropped him off and went to my job at the car dealership.

We visited my grandparents, mommy and poppy. I love them so. During the week we went to work, came home and went fishing so we would have something to eat. This was everyday. If we didn't catch fish we didn't eat. We always fished until we did catch some. We fried them up and ate them. I was so confused. How did I end up like this? We didn't have television or telephone. We went to bed at 8 o'clock and got up around four am. He had turned mean. One morning he took my hot rollers and threw them and broke my great grandmother's lamp. It was old and I was so sad.

After I dropped him off I drove to Mommy and Poppy's house but it was early. I didn't want to wake them up. I just sat in my car in front of their house and cried. I cried for about an hour. I left because I didn't want to be late for work. I should have gone to the door.

The man I married was becoming mean. He told me he dreaded having sex with me. That was it for me. I went to my mother and told her what he said. She said go get my things and come stay with her in her one bedroom apartment. I did. She had a date so she left and my husband at the time came to the door. I let him in. Next we moved into a two bedroom house made of rocks.

Evan locked me outside in my underwear for about an hour. I cried and I talked to God. I told God I needed my Daddy. I begged for my Daddy to help me. That's the only way I knew of that I could get away from this mean person. My cat, Sheeba, got very sick. The vet didn't know what was wrong with him but he didn't respond to any treatment. I worked at a car dealership close to the vet's office and went on my lunch hour to hold him. I would cry and rock him. The vet finally told me he was suffering and it would be best to put him to sleep. Evan made me get him from the vet and bring him home. He suffered and died two nights later. I could hear him crying as I lay in bed. I was in a bad place mentally. I knew the one thing that I loved with all my heart was dying and I couldn't go to him because I was afraid. I'd never seen anyone die. He cried out for the last time about two o'clock in the morning. I knew he was dead. When Evan woke up I told him Sheeba was dead. I didn't know what to do with his body. Evan took me into the woods with Sheeba in a black garbage bag and I laid him on a mountain in the sunshine. I was in shock and I cried for so long my face was swelled up for two days. I continued to cry everyday.

Evan hollered all the time. I wasn't accustomed to someone verbally abusing me. He would leave to go play poker every Saturday night. He left me alone every chance he got. My sister had come to stay with me. She saw how he was treating me. My daddy came for a visit soon after my sister left. He found the kitchen window covered with a garbage bag because he had thrown the telephone through the window. My sister must have told my daddy about him pulling me around by the hair, etc.

Chapter 8

MY DADDY CALLED me one day and said he didn't like to break up marriages but that he wanted to come get me and take me to Arkansas so I could go to college. I did. I felt my prayer had been answered from the night I was locked outside in my underwear.

The plan was for my Daddy to come right after Evan left for work. That day my Daddy pulled in. He had a shot gun. The first and only time I've seen him with a gun. He told my stepbrother and my brother to load up in a hurry.

We were through and gone by the time the mean bastard got there. Someone had called him at work and told him what was going on. We barely missed him. The van was borrowed from one of my stepbrother's friend who had a band. I'm not too sure if it ran very well, but we made it to Arkansas. I stayed with my Daddy and stepmother for a while and then he moved me on campus.

I got divorced. I started class. I felt out of place and like I was dressed wrong. I had no clothes to speak of. I was in a small town, dry county and living alone for the first time in my life. I had a neighbor who loved to party so I went along with her.

I dated a guy whose father was an accounting teacher and I thought I would like accounting. I made A's. He took me to meet his parents. We didn't last long.

I kept running into a guy that was on a baseball scholarship. He wasn't much to look at in the face but he had a body that wouldn't quit. He also had a way about him that made him interesting. He had a great sense of humor. We ended up in Physical Science class together. He didn't sit with me at first. He was one of those that chasing him would run him off. He had attitude. I liked him. He went to High School with a girl that was also in our class. She would come to class and see him sitting beside me and leave. She was interested and I think they had something going on in High School. He picked me. Our first date was when I got home and on the door was a note that said "Gone to Memphis. I'm on a business with some friends. I thought so this is the way it's going to be.

I got to class before him and he would come sat by me. I talked to him and acted like nothing ever happened. I didn't say anything about the note or the date. I acted like nothing happened. He wanted to know if I wanted to buy the answers to the test we were taking the next day. I said no. I paid attention in class and did my homework. The next day we took the test. He used his bought answers and I answered because I knew the answers. When he saw my B and his F he decided he would copy my answers. He came by and he took me places. We smoked pot together. When it snowed he would stay. I would make stew and we would play cards. I still wasn't hanging on his every word and this confused him. I think he thought I should be honored that he was in my presence.

If he told me he would call me at 8 o'clock and it got to be one minute after 8 I would go out with my girlfriend that lived down the street. If he said he'd be there at 9 and he wasn't there at 9 I wasn't at home. I went out. No one had ever done this before. I kept it up for four months. I went on a trip to Alabama and went to an Alabama, Auburn game with the man who made such sweet love to me. He still wanted me. I made a mistake leaving him and I didn't realize I had. One of the bad things about being Bi-Polar.

We also went to a Journey concert. We had a great time. My cousin that abandoned me went. We spoke a few times but nothing has ever been the same between us. I knew she would always tell me if something wasn't right or didn't look good. She ended up having an Interior Design business in Birmingham and marrying an attorney. I wonder if he knows she's bisexual and hit on me two times. Anyway, back to Mr. Baseball.

When I got home he came over. He told me he loved me in his own way the first time by touching his eye, his heart and pointed at me. That meant I love you. I told him I loved him too. After that we were together all the time. I got pregnant and we got married. My daddy gave me $500 for the wedding. I bought another ugly blue dress, it was on sale cheap. I was shopping with his brother's wife. She was a lovely person but she shouldn't have let me buy that dress. We had a ceremony in my daddy's living room. We had some guests present. We had a cake. We were supposed to go to an amusement park, I don't remember where. Instead we went home. I don't remember if we had sex. He didn't know about foreplay and was one of the worst lovers I have ever had. I know his car wasn't running right. It turned out it needed water in the radiator.

He graduated barely. He was on academic probation until the semester he graduated with a Degree in Psychology and a 2.0 grade point average. We celebrated his graduation with another couple. He had barely made it out also. He had to mount a fish for one point for one of his professors. Grandma and Grandpa kept the kids that night.

We had three children. We lived in Tennessee for his job. He became an insurance salesman. He worked long hours. I kept the children. Then we moved to Georgia. I had suspected he was cheating on me for a long time. One night the babysitter and our son heard on the phone with a woman after twelve pm. I was in bed asleep. It was hard to keep everything attended to and as close to perfect as anybody could. My husband and my family were my life and I loved my life. I did until I woke the next morning and I was told what had gone on the night before.

I was reading a magazine and saw an advertisement for a car that I thought was beautiful. I showed it to my husband and we were at the car lot three hours later buying one. I thought this is a great guilt gift. I still held my tongue. This was my life and I didn't want my life to end up in the toilet.

I had my suspicions so I got the baby sitter to sit with the kids. I went out and looked around. I went to the pool hall he was always sneaking off to on Sundays. I would look up and he would be gone. I walked in. I went to him. He said I was tired and should probably go home. I noticed a couple of rough looking girls over in the back corner watching me. He gave me a one hundred dollar bill—I called them pictures of Ben. I said ok and left to go home. I was watching and noticed I was being followed. They followed me all the way home and turned around in the driveway when I pulled into the garage.

I arranged for marriage counseling. He attended but did nothing but sit there with a smirk on his face. He did that three times.

He left whenever he wanted to. He didn't want to participate. He was done with me. The marriage counselor asked me if there was anything he could do that would make me want to make love to him. I said "No". He wasn't any good anyway. Get it and go was his way. He was so bad that when I asked him to rub my back he said he would if I would blow him. Foreplay was a concept l ost on him. Anyway the counselor said "You should save yourself some grief and get divorced."

I left her office and went to the bank. I took all the money out of our savings account. The next morning at seven am I was waiting on him. I was awake and at the foot of the stairs when he walked in promptly at seven am. He headed for the stairs and I told him he didn't live here anymore. I had his 357 loaded to prove it. He got mad and went upstairs and called his mommy to tell her I had a loaded gun. She must have told him to leave the house because he did. On his way out I told him to come back at 5o'clock to get his clothes. He did and I gave him his clothes neatly in a suitcase. I don't know why I was so nice about the whole thing.

I hired the best divorce lawyer in town that afternoon. I ended up with full custody of the children, the house, and my car, everything we owned. He got nothing.

He didn't pay his child support so my Daddy paid the lawyer for a court order to garnish his check. I got my $250 every Saturday until he quit his job. Then my Daddy paid for an order to put him in jail. All I had to do was take it to my attorney and he would be arrested. The only problem was I couldn't execute the document. I couldn't put him in jail. I apologize to my Daddy for spending the money and taking the time to get the court order. I still loved him. That is so sad for me.

Chapter 9

I STARTED GOING to the only club in town. It was a stinky little town and now I was stuck there. When we moved there my then husband promised it would only be for two years. Now it was forever and I was stuck in the arm pit of a dirty little town with dirty little cops and politicians.

I was popular probably for the same reasons I was all those years before, my legs and my height. My hair and my face are attractive. Add my personality to the mix and you've got quite a catch.

Stupid, (my nickname for this ex), was bringing the children home. He had a black woman with him when he came to get the children. I was shocked and devastated. I found out she was a 57 year old black woman and I was over the edge of sanity. My Bi-Polar kicked in like a champ. I was all over the map.

Anyway, Stupid wanted to know where all the men came from and I wanted to know where the black woman came from, the 57 year old black woman. I found out where she came from. I also found out where he had spent all those nights. She seemed rather proud of herself when I met her. Her name was Willie. Willie, she was the 57 year old married black woman. Free Willie.

I asked Stupid not to bring her when he came to pick up the kids. They were embarrassed. I told the kids when they were with her and their father to act like she was their maid/care taker. She did cook for them and treated them good.

This woman had been in our bed. She had toured our house, my house, the place where I cooked and cleaned and cared for my children. The children told me they had seen her before when I was gone to a wedding out of town. Their daddy had told them she was a client and he had taken her to cash her check. I put it all together and I was livid. I was so far from rational thinking that it wasn't even funny. I was having a nervous breakdown and maybe due bipolar problem. I hadn't been diagnosed as Bipolar yet though. No one knew why I was doing what I was doing. My daddy was there for me financially. Other than that I was on my own.

I had the babysitter, a college girl that had problems with her mother, move in. She could care for the children when I went out. She could go to classes during the day while the children were in school.

It was the beginning of the summer so I decided to not go to work right away. I went to the swimming pool at the dinky little country club. I realized that I was stuck in the stinky little armpit of a town.

The swimming pool was clean. We went every day. The children loved every minute of it and I didn't mind laying in the sun drinking lemonade and rum with cherries. I wasn't lacking for the company of men or guys. Some guys are just guys and men, real men are hard to come by. I met one man at the neighbor's house. They had invited me over to play cards. I drank beer and played cards. The man they introduced me to was ok. He worked for Georgia Power. I didn't know him very well having just met. He did take me home and I passed out on the couch. He was still there the next morning when I woke up. He asked me if I was ok. I told him yes and wondered why he was still in my house. He was still in my house because he had set his sights on me. I was to be his is what he was thinking. He was a good guy and I dated him for a couple of months. By the end of the summer he proposed to me. I don't know why but I said yes. I guess because he had a good job, and he was stable and he wanted to marry me. That would solve all my problems. I wouldn't lose my house. I would just move him in and he could take Stupid's place.

He took me to the jewelry store and bought me a small marquise shaped diamond ring. He said he would get me a bigger one later. I didn't like the ring and I was embarrassed it was so small. I put it on anyway. He went to my house and told my children we were engaged. He took us all to Chick Filet to eat our engagement dinner. I was under whelmed.

I didn't get mad until he came in the quick mart I was working at and pretended not to know me. He said nothing to me. I guess he was embarrassed I was working at the quick mart. It was at the end of the street so I got a job there while I looked for a full time job somewhere. I was qualified to do any job I wanted so I wasn't worried. I got unengaged from him.

I got a job at a tax software company. I had to be there evenings.

We all had to attend a training class. The teacher had the hots for me. Everyone in the class told me he liked me. I looked at him and decided he was ok looking and he had to be intelligent. It turned out he was also a DJ at the local country station. How special. I was intrigued. He asked me if he could come over to my house after work. I told him it was my daughter's birthday and I would be having a party for her but he could come over about 10 o'clock and bring some beer. He was just right on time.

After everyone was in bed I talked to him. I found out he was nine years younger than me. At first to me that was a deal breaker but I found out he was a computer nerd and made enough money to fill Stupid's shoes so he became a contender.

Just for kicks I was also seeing a big guy who played in a band at the only bar in town. He fixated on me and during the break he asked me to dance. I figured he was interested in getting in my pants so while we were dancing I informed him I would not sleep with him because I didn't sleep with anyone unless I was married to them. There I was again with the M word. He told me he was a DEA agent too.

I was told to be careful because there were lots of DEA agents in this town because there was a huge drug problem just over the Georgia Alabama state line. I believed that. Somehow I managed to string the Georgia Power man along and the DJ guy while I was seeing the DEA man. He had a massage table in his house. I was always tense and I loved a good massage so if I wasn't busy somewhere else I would go to his house for a massage.

I don't know how I managed to do all this. My kids were in bed before I left the house. I came home at night so I would be there when they woke up. I would take them to school and do whatever I was doing until time to pick them up from school. They were doing fine with the situation. My diabetic son had some rage or something. One day he was chasing my middle daughter through the house with a huge knife in his hand. I decided it would be better for a boy to be with the daddy. I called Stupid and told him what was going on and he agreed. We took our son to Shoney's to tell him. He looked so happy to be alone with us. I can still remember the look on his face when we told him he would be going to live with his father. His father was still living with Free Willie. My son broke that up. He didn't want his friends to come over and see a black woman in the house.

I was happy that Willie was gone. The woman had the nerve to try to be my friend. We went to lunch together and discussed my children, etc. I did not know what to think about a thirty three year old guy was doing with a 57 year old woman whether she was black or white. I didn't know what to think and to this day I don't know what to think about that situation. It was the biggest insult to me. I'm still waiting on Stupid to apologize to me for destroying our happy home.

I try to get him every time I have a chance. I want an apology and I will continue to be a pain in his ass until he apologizes to me.

When Stupid decided after two years to break it off with Willie she called me to complain about Stupid and how he had hurt her. I pacified her and listened to her. I finally told her what she expected. He had broken up a thirteen year marriage with me. He was just bad news and she should have never thought that she would be with him forever. I was very insulted that she would call me to discuss her breakup with the father of my children.

Anyway, I was still playing with all three of these guys. DJ and Georgia Power knew about each other. The DEA guy didn't know about Georgia Power and the DJ and they didn't know about the DEA guy.

The only time I ever tried to buy marijuana by myself I got it from the DEA guy. I had half the money that night and I told him I would give him the rest the next day. Little did I know that his interest in me was actually an attempt to bust me. I had avoided that situation by not having all the money at one time. Later he told me what he was doing and how he had busted other women that way and that he got in trouble for not being able to bust me.

Then he got serious about me. He came to my house all the time. He was always telling us we passed some kind of test required for the wife of a DEA agent. I guess he thought I was going to marry him. I never said yes or no. I avoided the whole situation. For one thing he had a child and I wanted to avoid the whole stepmother situation. I had a stepmother and I learned that I didn't want to be anyone's stepmother from her. I just couldn't be mean enough to be a stepmother. I wasn't up to the task. Hurting people was not on my list of things to do.

Anyway back to the story of my Bi-Polar life. It was fall and I was still talking to the Georgia Power Guy and the DJ guy. In the meantime I managed to date the Jewish man. He had been a client of the accountant I had worked for briefly. He let me go when my son was diagnosed as diabetic. That was so sweet of him after that big test his wife had put me through during her interview. What a waste of skin.

The Jewish man was a lot of fun. He came in the only club in town one night. I was there with the girls from the City Attorney law firm I worked at until I quit to go to work for the Accountant. I was bored at the attorney's office. All I did was transcribe notes for two associates that I didn't think were very intelligent and didn't think had much of future with this law firm. They were playing with the big ole boys.

The Jewish guy saw me. I was dressed to kill in a black dress that fit just so and black hills. He came over and asked me to dance. It was late so we didn't stay there long. He took me to the waffle house to eat. I wasn't hungry but I was curious. What was his agenda? He hung out at a bar in a hotel all the time. He was friends with the owner so we could drink all we wanted and stay in a room until we were sober enough to drive. I enjoyed his company. We would go to the room and talk and laugh and have fun. We never had sex and he told me if I told anyone we didn't have sex he would deny it. One night the night guard came by and knocked on the door and told us to hold it down. We thought that was funny. I became known as the Jewish guy's girlfriend at that bar.

It turned out he was using me somehow to move cocaine. That's where the DEA agent came into my life. They thought I was moving cocaine. I had never seen cocaine much less used cocaine. I was investigated thoroughly according to the DEA guy.

While the Jewish guy was using me he developed feelings for me. He told me he could never marry me because I wasn't Jewish. I didn't want to marry him anyway. There was the M word again. What was I, the marrying kind? Why did all these guys think I was going to even think about marrying them?

I still didn't realize who I was. I had low self esteem from years of mistreatment from my mother and my daddy was at work all the time. He later told me it was a good thing he was at work all the time or he wouldn't have the money to support me. He said he sold his vacation time to have the money to support me and my stepmother could never know. No one could ever know what he did for me. I love him so much and I wanted to know who he was, what he liked, what he didn't like. I wanted to know him. I wanted to spend time with him. I'm a big ole daddy's girl. Always have been, always will be.

Back to my bipolar life. I was let go by the tax software company and I didn't really care. I couldn't explain to tax people how to use this program. I didn't learn anything because the teacher was hot for me. He chased me like a dog. I dated the Georgia Power man and the DJ guy that was also the tax software teacher. It was fall still and I had decided to go to the Georgia Power man's house. The DJ guy followed us. We went in the house. He pulled into the driveway and started hollering for me to come out. He carried a gun and I didn't know what he was doing. I was amused by this situation until I heard a gunshot. I was scared then. I could see me explaining to his mom that he shot himself because I wouldn't come outside. I told the Georgia Power man to go see if the DJ guy has shot himself. He went out there and the DJ guy was lying on the ground. The Georgia Power man looked at him and he had not shot himself. The Georgia Power man told him to get up and go home or somewhere else. I was so glad the DJ guy hadn't shot himself. He finally got in his car and left.

The Georgia Power man took me out to eat. We had a nice dinner and went back to his house. It was time for me to go home so I left. He wanted me to come back the next day so I did. There was a huge hail storm and my car was destroyed by the hail. They fixed it but it wasn't exactly the color it had been. It was a little bluer than it had been. It looked ok. At least it was restored. I was in the wrong place at the wrong place at the wrong time. The Geogia Power man wanted to marry me. It was January of the year. He wanted to go to Gatlinburg and get married so we did. In January during a snow storm with the roads closed. I didn't know the roads were closed until we got there. The guilt gift Intrepid makes it over the ice and snow like it was nothing. When we got home I was informed by the live in baby sitter who called me "mom" by this time, informed me of the DJ guy's reaction to me eloping with the Power man. He sat at my house for a whole day lamenting my quick marriage to the Power man.

We checked into a nice hotel and the next day we went to a wedding chapel and were married. We got the package that included pictures. I wore jeans and a sweater that I wore only once and that was to get married. After the ceremony we went to a nice restaurant and had dinner. We had a hot tub in the room and we bought bubble bath and hit the Jacuzzi. He was pretty good in bed. Now I had someone I could depend on. When we got home I stopped at florets to get a white ribbon to put on the mailbox to symbolize that I had gotten married. We had a big reception party. My mother and sister were there. The couple that introduced us attended. His old roommate attended. My children were there. It was a party. We had a cake, I don't know if it was a wedding cake. He mashed cake all over my face and I got mad. That embarrassed me. I didn't want cake all over my face, in my opinion that was an indication of disrespect.

He turned out to be a speed freak. He had a weight problem. He worked two weeks on each of the three shifts. That probably explains how I was able to string along the DJ and the DEA guy. We were "happy" until about the third week when he came home from first shift and had a cold. He took out his partial, lay down on the bed and asked me for a Xanax so he could sleep. The whole picture depressed me and made me mad at the same time. He was a penny pinching man.

It turns out that I wasn't too happy. He tried to pick my son up by the throat because he was sitting in the rocking recliner watching television. The grouchy man shouldn't have tried to pick up my son by the throat. I could put up with a lot of things but not being mean and hurtful to my son.

We rocked along for about a week longer so that would make a month. By this time I was really disappointed. Being married to him was nothing like Stupid. I was trying to replace Stupid. That's what Bi-Polar people do. We do lots of things that don't make sense to non Bi-Polar people. I still wasn't diagnosed. I had been going to the Psychiatrist for years by this time. He said I was in situational depression. I paid cash and he scheduled my appointments at three month intervals. I had stopped going to him at this time.

I didn't tell anyone I had gotten married. I didn't tell the girl who cuts my hair, anyone. They all knew because of an insert in the paper that told all the dirt on everyone. No one asked and I didn't tell. Four weeks does not a marriage make?

We got to the droll existence part way too fast. He had begun to sleep instead of having a good time, he was grouchy and I didn't like this whole situation and him. One night I hadn't given it much thought but I swallowed a lot of Xanax and several, a lot, of some muscle relaxer I took because my neck burned and hurt and swallowed them in a dash. I saved some Xanax and hid them. I knew, from my mother's attempts, that you couldn't always count on not waking up.

After I took the pills I thought of my children and told him I had inadvertently taken too many pills. I had thought I would just go to sleep and never wake up again. But then what would happen to my kids. He got up and took me to the hospital. I was still awake until we got to triage. I fell over and was out until two days later. When I came to I had been hooked up to a respirator. They took it out.

The first thing I saw was my mother. She asked me why I had done this. That was the first question I heard after I came to when the doctor wasn't too hopeful I would make. Someone had called my Daddy. He was at the hospital too. That afternoon I was released. I saw my Daddy. His first sentence was "I was in Germany for work and it cost me a lot of money to fly here." None of these statements the first time I was alert were very good for me emotionally. I don't remember what Power guy said. This exciting turn of events had made me feel washed out, sad. I hadn't accomplished anything. I had succeeded in being embarrassed to the 9th power and that was all I had done. I had cost my Daddy a lot of money and my mother was tired from sitting at the hospital wondering if I would recover. The hospital had discharged me without a referral to a psychiatrist, literally all I had done was humiliate myself. The only reaction to this whole event was morbid humiliation.

Thank God my children knew nothing. They had been told I was ill and that was all. I started in on my destructive thinking. The day after I got out of the hospital and supposedly rejoined the thinking world we went out to breakfast with my Daddy and my stepmother. They all made meaningless small talk and I was still embarrassed.

On Saturday I took off in my car. I had some beer and I was just driving and thinking. I had left my daddy at home to break the news to Power man that I wanted him to move out, take all his trifling furniture and get out of my house. Not once did I have a rational thought.

When I got home power man was gone. His furniture was still in my house. My daddy was still there and told me that he never wanted to break up for me again. Apparently there was a strong reaction to this news. He wasn't Bi-Polar and he didn't understand. Neither do I.

I called the DJ guy. I told him I had tried to kill myself because I had married the wrong man. I told him I was actually in love with him. Almost before I hung up the phone he was there with me. He had no questions. He needed no explanation. He had me now and that's all he was concerned about.

I drank beer and he drove. He loved his car and wanted to go anywhere as long as he was driving his Mustang. He was a member of the Mustang Club. One spring day we attended the Mustang Club's cookout. It was a boring event that turned out to be hilarious. All these men and their Mustang's were attempting to make grilled hot dogs. The only thing they did wrong was forget anything to make a fire to grill them on.

I wish you could have seen these men, with their big Mustangs, try to figure out how to grill the hot dogs. I was trying my best not to laugh. They finally decided to gather up some twigs, very small pieces of wood and some leaves to start the fire. It didn't start a good fire but nevertheless they put those hot dogs on the grill and "cooked" them. I was just glad they hadn't decided on hamburgers for this over rated phallic symbol outing. The only thing they cared about was who had the best "Mustang". The whole thing was crazy funny to me. The DJ's guy had a friend that owned a Saleen Mustang. That was a very big deal because some guy named Saleen had trimmed it out and signed his name on the dashboard. He didn't turn out many per year so they were numbered. They were also expensive—at least $50 thousand or more if it was a particularly good tricked out one.

There are two people I've always wanted to meet. The Saleen guy that tricked out these cars and signed them and David Letterman. I want to talk to David Letterman and find out how to get paid for being a smart ass.

The DJ guy and I were engaged. I picked out my engagement ring and traded the one Stupid had bought me when I was pregnant with our third child. I loved the ring and thought it was big enough. It didn't say "I saved up my beer money and bought you this ring." It was just over one carat.

I was working through a temporary agency at the Planning Commission. I was filling in for the Executive Secretary with Carpal Tunnel. I did such a good job they decided to add me as an employee of the Planning Commission.

DJ and I were married the first of July. That made two marriages in one year. The ceremony was held at the Historical Society in the gardens. We had hired a caterer for the event. My mother and sister attended wearing white dresses. They didn't know it was socially unacceptable to attend a wedding in white dresses. His family were there and my mother and sister.

I wore a white wedding gown with a train like one I had seen in a Bridal magazine. I kept the magazine. It was a beautiful dress. I had made dresses like mine for my daughters. My soon to be mother in law made one and I made one. We sewed for the afternoon and the dresses were done. She was an excellent seamstress.

She said her ring looked like a baby from my ring. I knew what the meaning of that statement was. She thought I had robbed her son. She didn't know that I had traded in Stupid's ring and that took the cost down by one half.

After the reception, an uncomfortable and embarrassing situation took place. My mother and sister were on one side of the room and DJ guy and his family was on the other side of the reception room. We had a beautiful wedding cake and it tasted very good also. The DJ guy insisted that he have the sausages in barbeque sauce. The reception was pulled off by the caterer. After what seemed like a long time we left for our honeymoon. His mustang had white balloons tied to it and Just Married written on the back windshield and the windows on the doors. When we left the reception he had to make his drive through town. Thank God it was a small town and didn't take long.

We left for our honeymoon in a rather large city. We had a suite. He made love to me for two days. I could have an orgasm with him so this was great. He was intelligent enough to have an intelligent conversation with. That was refreshing. We went on a showboat dinner trip. The dinner wasn't very good and the entertainment was worse. When it was finally over we returned to the historical hotel and to our suites. We spent two days on our honeymoon. We were supposed to be there three days but my mother was watching my children and I was worried what she was doing with them. My new husband had no problem with cutting the honeymoon short.

When we got home I walked through the door and my son was lighting fire crackers in the house. My mother was reading as usual. The house was destroyed. We let her go home. She was actually supposed to live with us. She was having problems living with my sister and her husband and two children in a cramped two bedroom trailer.

I was mad because my children were lighting firecrackers in the house and my mother went back to the trailer with my sister, her husband and their two kids. There were a couple of dogs and a cat. My sister can't go a day without having a dog or two. The more dogs she had made her happier.

The DJ had taken out a loan to catch up the house payments. It was Thanksgiving and Stupid brought me some skunk marijuana back for me. I didn't think DJ guy would mind. He had taken me to his cousins to smoke. He had no problem with me smoking.

After the children were asleep I rolled one and went downstairs to smoke. DJ guy went to pieces. He had made a tape with my movie camera composed of where I had hidden the marijuana. I called my mother because he was out of control. He was livid. My mother got to me at a record speed. It was an hour drive at least. She told me on the phone to flush the pot and I did. Then she broke up the fight and destroyed the video tape evidence. By this time it was about six am. DJ guy went to his parent's house and told them what I had tried to do.

At about eight am they showed up with the truck and moved his bed and everything he owned. It wasn't a lot. His mother demanded I take off my rings and give them to her. I was crying and I gave them to her. I cried all that day. My mother took me to the doctor and they gave me some medication that calmed me down and I finally stopped crying. I was in a whirlwind. I couldn't think and didn't want to.

Somehow DJ guy got the check that had been credited to the house payments and got it reversed. When the check came back it had paid stamped on it and he had the money back.

My daddy told me to find a house to rent and he would pay for the furniture to be moved. He also put me in a hotel with my girls for two weeks under his business name. He didn't want DJ man to hurt me and they were afraid he would. He stalked me. He would be at the school when I dropped my children off in the morning. Where ever I went he was there. He had followed me to the hotel. He had bribed the desk clerk and went I got back from getting the children after work we got something to eat the desk clerk told me that something had been left at the desk for me. It was a six pack of beer. My daddy told me to hurry and rent a house so I could escape from him.

I rented a house out of the city for $350 a month. It didn't have a shower and it turned out not to be in the school district I thought it was. My children were called preps because they had clothes that were nice and I fixed their long curly, beautiful hair every morning. I put a bow in their hair like always. I had a very small bedroom and their bedroom had a door to the outside. This house had two front porch doors. I decorated it and it looked good. I had a dining room of sorts, a living room and the kitchen didn't have a dishwasher. I had rented this house to save my Daddy money. He told me he would help me and I was trying to save him money. In retrospect I knew I should have rented a house in the small neighbor had Garden Lakes not far from the children's school. I would have been happier and probably wouldn't have gone and tried to make it work with DJ guy.

A couple of weeks went by. I called Power man and he was right there for me. He started being at my house every minute he could. Meanwhile DJ man was threatening to kill me and was still stalking me. One day Power man and I were going somewhere and DJ guy was following us. We stopped at a red light and a police car was behind us. I ran for the police car, got in the back and told the police man that the husband I was separated from was stalking me and trying to kill me. The police man drove me to a nearby school lot. The school wasn't in session because it was Saturday. Power man and DJ man pulled into the parking lot. The police man told DJ man to stop following me or he would go to jail. He left and I got back in the truck with Power man.

Valentine's Day came and I was seeing DJ guy and Power man at the same time. I saw DJ guy while Power man was at work. When Valentine's Day came I was not feeling well and called in sick. The children were at school and I was in the bed. Bi-Polar was rearing its ugly head again.

I got a call from the florist asking for directions to my house because they had a delivery for me. Power man learned that I was seeing DJ guy and cancelled the flowers. DJ guy came over for Valentine's Day and brought me and my girl's candy. I wanted roses. DJ guy had once sent me a dozen red roses. I counted them as I always did and instead of a dozen there were eleven. The card read "You're the twelfth rose." I was very impressed.

DJ guy and I got back together. He got my rings back from his mother and we moved into his duplex with him. It had two bedrooms and two bathrooms so it was perfect for us. Stupid had come to help DJ guy move my things. Stupid ended up with my new refrigerator after my son told me theirs didn't work right and didn't keep things cold. I sold my washer and dryer and all the things in the storage room. That included a lead crystal chandelier that I loved. There were many good things in there and he gave me two hundred and fifty dollars for everything.

There was a box of pictures that had been put in that room that I didn't know about. He brought the pictures to my office at the Planning Commission. By this time my mentally handicapped hair lipped boss was recording his thoughts about my employment performance and things about personal conversations I had with Stupid over my son's school problems. Power guy and were divorced in March and I was planning a wedding to DJ guy for July 2. I got married twice in one year. Trying to replace Stupid had taken its toll on me and neither on of them replaced Stupid. DJ guy was pretty good in bed and Power guy wasn't after we were married. Before Power Guy and I got married he had been pretty good but after the ceremony went all the good things he did. He counted himself as living in my house and telling everyone, including me, what to do.

DJ guy and I got back together. We bought a house with a pool. Everything was going fine. My son was with his dad and my daughters were with me and DJ guy. I got dismissed from my job because DJ guy called and told them I smoked pot. Then we lost a sizeable amount of money each month. It was missed. DJ guy got mad because Stupid wasn't paying his child support and a check bounced. He ranted and raved for hours. My mother was supposed to pick up the children so they wouldn't see this mess. Finally I got mad enough and left with a base ball bat. He had a gun. It was Good Friday, Easter was Sunday. I didn't have any money so I sold my engagement ring for $400 to get the children Easter dresses and the Easter Bunny things.

We were staying with my sister. We stayed there about five days and were sick of the dogs and the dog poop everywhere. My sister is happy without a bunch of dogs in the house. We went to stay with my mother in her trailer. All my fears about divorcing Stupid had happened. We now lived with my mother in Payne Mobile Home Park. I was in pain and sick about this turn of events. The next Saturday I rented a U Haul and went to the house to get my furniture and things. I got everything except the dishes and pots and pans my mother was supposed to pack and forgot. I lost all my favorite recipes, everything for the kitchen except the knick knacks and decorations for the kitchen.

My Uncle, my mother's brother, hired to guys that lived across from him in the trailer park. One was old and crazy and the other was about my age, an Italian. He worked with a man installing floors. I decided I liked him. Eventually my mother had him move in and pay $100 a week to live there. She finally had pimp me out. I know she was happy about that. She tried with the Alabama Power man and that didn't fly. Now I was at the bottom of the barrel in more ways than one, a new time low.

I felt sorry for the moving guy. He had lost his three children because of crack cocaine. He didn't do that anymore or so I thought. I know he didn't do it so that I knew. He had always wanted a girl like me. I was attracted to him. After about two months we decided to move to Florida and rent a house and get his kids out of Foster Care. That was easy enough. All three of them were there and all three of my children were there. His children were wild and weird. I guess that's what happens in Foster Care. His daughter was a lesbian. His son was a Goth weirdo and his other son was slick. He had me liking him.

Moving guy got a job at a Pizzeria. He had experience. He made specialty pizzas. I tried delivering pizzas but not being familiar with the area I wasn't very good at that. I would take my daughters with me. I didn't want them around his kids. I don't remember ever making over fifteen dollars in tips and I had a 1999 Chrysler Sebring. It was my favorite car I ever had. It was beautiful and it would fly.

Pizza Man had to be at work at 9:00 am and got off at 10:00 pm. We didn't see each other much. The children were in two bedrooms, three to a room. The rooms weren't large.

One night Pizza man told me he didn't like my kids, his children didn't like my kids or me. Then he went to sleep. I got up and went into the living room. We lived fifteen minutes from the ocean. I love the ocean.

It came time to enroll the children in school. There was a nice school right in the neighborhood but you had to be on a waiting list for years to go to that school. They intended to ship my daughters to a school all the way across town to a bad school with armed guards. I couldn't let that happen. I called Stupid and told him he would have to take the girls so they would be in a good school. He said he would. The next Saturday I met him at the Miami Zoo and let him take my precious daughters away. I knew it was best for them but the whole ride home I don't remember and I cried all the way. My children, my precious daughters were my life. My life had no meaning without them. I felt numb, I felt like I had failed them. I didn't feel good about this at all and I thought I was no good to them. I still had my son and that was good. I loved him. He was my first born.

I became depressed and didn't think life was worth living. My son was in Rome Georgia for a Court hearing. He had flown out Friday afternoon. He was supposed to fly back on Wednesday. I was still thinking of the pizza man and what he had said to me about not liking my children. None of my children were in Florida. I had been going to the ocean and writing on a suicide note for about a week. I had dated it each time I wrote. I had verbiage for my Daddy, my mother, and my children. I finally decided everyone would be better off if I was dead. I was a failure. I took enough Xanax for a good nap. I didn't have that many. The next morning his children found my note and my instructions about Brandon not getting on the plane to come back.

I was taken to the hospital, my stomach was pumped and I was full of charcoal. I couldn't believe it when I woke up. There is nothing worse than thinking you will never wake up again and waking up. I felt stupid. I felt awful. I was really humiliated. After I woke up good the nurse said I had to go to a mental hospital for 72 hours. It was the law in Florida. A policeman came and took me in the backseat of his car. I didn't have to wear handcuffs.

This state run hospital wasn't bad. I had a room with another girl and we shared a bathroom. I don't remember much. I called my sister and mother and they arranged to come and get me. Pizza man had called my

Daddy and told him to come get me. He paid for a U Haul, my brother came from Kentucky, and my mother came from Georgia. My first visit with the doctor consisted of me telling him my family was coming to get me. He signed a release but I don't think he really believed me. That afternoon they were there. We went to eat and then we went to the house and packed up all my things, including kitchen ware, everything except a plant I had had for 17 years. It was huge and my brother had already hurt his back with my Great Grandfather's chest of drawers. I said I had to leave the plant. He just couldn't pick it up. I felt bad he had hurt his neck.

We were packed in about two hours and made it back to Georgia the next day. We spent the night in a hotel. They had been driving all day from early in the morning. By eight o'clock everything was on the truck and we were out of there. Pizza man came to the Pharmacy and told me he didn't mean the things he had said that night. My brother saw me talking to him and hollered "Debra, get away from that piece of shit.

We got back to Georgia and all my things were put in storage.

Again, I was in the trailer park with my mother. After a long bout with depression I got a job at an insurance company. I was a good agent and every week I was number one with production. I had women that had been there fifteen years wanting to ride with me and see what I was doing to make all these sales.

I had met a guy at a local club I went to listen to music. When I walked in the door there was a six foot four inch man with long blonde hair. He was sexy and I had always wanted to date a guy with long hair. I walked right up to him and started talking. He ended up going to the box with me and we slept on the couch. I had had three shots of tequila and I was out.

We dated for over a year. He was an automotive technician and made excellent money. He bought me anything I wanted. For Valentine's Day he special ordered me some roses, gave me a diamond heart necklace and a negligent. I had a great Valentine's Day. My mother had a horrible day and was jealous of me and the mechanic.

About a week later I didn't have to go into the office because I had number one production. I was waking up about 10:00. I heard the phone ring, I heard my mother answer questions about where I worked and everything they wanted to know. Then she came to my bedroom door and said in this tone of voice "Debra, I think I just made a mistake. I thought mechanic man wanted to send you something to work."

With Pizza Man I couldn't make the payments on the Sebring so I returned it to a dealership in Florida. Payday came and I didn't have a direct deposit. I had a check for $50.00 my check had been garnished. I didn't see any way to keep my money and my mother had done this on purpose. Every time I am happy and doing well she does something to blow up my life. Every single time. I don't know why she hates me so much.

About a month after that I was told by my mother my Daddy had bought me a trailer in Payne Mobile Home Park I was also told my stepmother bought it for my mother. All I know is I lived there and paid the taxes.

I was lived by myself for five years in a trailer my Daddy bought me for $2500.00 in Payne Mobile Home Park. My Uncle, my mother's brother, had a carpet and flooring business. He lived two trailers down and liked to drink a lot. He still does. My Uncle helped me paint and clean the trailer. He put in new carpet and a new kitchen floor. He put in a new bathroom floor also. When I moved in it was like new. I had nice, expensive furniture, art and what knots. I had a very nice home. I enjoyed living by myself very much. I washed clothes about every three weeks and I could go and come as I pleased.

I had a friend named Brenda. She was significantly older than me. We went out all the time. She talked me into breaking up with the sexy automotive technician. Then she got a boyfriend way out of league. She dropped me like a hot potato.

I met another guy at the same bar. He was ok looking but he had several screws loose it turned out. I was there about thirty minutes and he about tackled me leaving the bar. After that he was unshakeable. He drove me crazy and stole my Xanax. I learned to hide them very well. He thought he moved in but he didn't. He went to a ball game one day and he was already wacked out on pills. He got arrested and I had his family come and get his stuff out of my house.

When he got out of jail he still called me. He told me I was the only friend he had that he could talk to. I let him come over and ended up sending him back in a cab with ten dollars. For some reason I agreed to come to his brother's Super Bowl game. There I met the man that caused me more heartache than anyone I had ever met.

Chapter 10

I T ALL STARTED at a Super Bowl Party. I met Chief. He was short, bald, and over weight. I will be kind and not say he was fat.

His eyes twinkled. Everyone else left to do the drugs he had delivered to the party. I was sort of dating one of the participants in the drugs he delivered. I was left out thankfully. People with big drug problems are stingy. I would have left with Chief if he asked me. I didn't know he had delivered the drugs.

It would be one year and three months before I would cross paths with Chief again. He had the old friend with him for two days, the friend had stolen money for his brother and bought a car. Chief called to warn me and I was so mortified I left with Chief, a beer in one hand, a tank top and some shorts. I was buzzed because I'd been drinking beer. I had a drinking problem. I threw some stuff in a bag, my Mary Kay and Retin A and left. We had a good drive, we stopped by his brothers house. We also stopped at a hardware store and got a plumbing part. Something had burst and water was leaking bad. Andy fixed that. We also stopped at the store for some groceries and the quick mart so I could buy some beer.

Chapter 11

WE BEGAN BY spending the weekend together. He had a couple of friends over. One friend was kind enough to bring two freaky girls with him for some perverted sex. They left. The guys stayed and Chief cooked for us. He was a good cook. He smelt like roses. The guys talked and laughed, we smoked lots of good marijuana.

One of the guys told me a man got caught eating his wife right down the street. I thought "oh no here comes the filth and danger". The guy was serious. A man had his dead wife in the car and was literally eating her. Cannibalism as they said. It was a relief that it was not a dirty joke and I felt safe so I had a good time. Chief had to give me a warmer shirt. I didn't know the temperature was twenty degrees colder in the mountains. In the mountains where the fog isn't fog, it is clouds. It's really amazing and as a child I had been to this mountain and drove through the clouds. As an adult I had dreamed of the rocks and the confusing layout but this was the house I had dreamed of.

Chief didn't take very good care of the lake house his mother so generously let him live in. He broke windows and all three doors had been broken into when he forgot his keys. She paid all the bills. His mother is afraid of him. She made this arrangement with him so he wouldn't burn his sister's house down. His sister supposedly didn't pay for something he did to her house when he built it. He says he built that house, but knowing him he supervised.

He'll tell you he raised his brother and I guess he did. His brother is on the line for payback big time. Chief even did a popper, whatever that is, before going into a doctor's office and it caused his blood pressure to be in the three hundreds. The doctor said he might die. That cinched the deal. His brother was on the hook. Not only was Chief mean to what he say, he is a master manipulator.

He put himself in on Jim's plumbing business, or manipulated the situation so that he could take over. Make no mistake, if Chief is there Chief is in charge. I always liked bad boys, I mean a lot. You could put me in a room with one hundred men that were good men and one was a bad boy and I would pick the bad boy.

We slept in the same bed, but I kept all my clothes on. The next morning he wanted to have sex. I liked him a lot and had since I met him at the Super Bowl party. I was surprised he didn't get in touch with me before a year and three months went by. He smelled like roses, seriously roses and I love red roses. I was drawn to him like a fish to water.

Later he asked me if I wanted to hunt arrow heads and we did. I looked down and picked one up immediately standing on the sidewalk. It was really perfect and Chief was impressed. He kept the arrow head. We were through hunting arrow heads. We smoked pot and chilled the rest of the day. I did some raking. He was also feeding me the first Hydrocodone I was exposed to. I was drinking beer. My mother had advised, on more than one occasion, me to calm down go buy a six pack and I did. Alcoholism runs rampant in her side of the family. It calmed me down, and eventually I could drink anybody under the table.

On Sunday, after spending the weekend, Chief took me home. Before he took me home he took me to an expensive restaurant. The food was delicious and he let me drink all the beer I wanted. He drank tea. I wasn't dressed appropriately. I had to sit with my back to the wall. I wasn't used to being in public or a restaurant like that. It didn't bother Andy.

Andy began picking me up every Friday and we stayed at the lake until Sunday or Monday. One Friday when we got there a girl was there with her dog. She flirted with Andy and acted like I wasn't supposed to be there. She was married but she was still there. She asked me if I needed a ride home. I told her Andy picked me up and would take me home Sunday or Monday. She got her wet dog and got in her truck and left after I got the gun Andy had bought at a pawn shop in my name. I didn't know it was illegal. He did. There he was, manipulating me. I could have gotten in a lot of trouble. I think he used me more than he loved me.

Before we were together every weekend Andy went to a concert with this girl. She told me they slept in the same bed. That bothered me a little but we weren't a couple technically. Andy had taken laughing gas and balloons to the concert and sold them for twenty dollars each.

The police came in their room to see what was going on and they were smoking marijuana. They took Andy's bag and left. Andy didn't mind, he had more in the car. He got another bag and they smoked all night. That was a weekend that I had plans. I had my daughter's to spend time with. He met me at the service station where Stupid and I dropped off and picked up the girls at six o'clock that evening so I knew he had been thinking about me.

After they returned from the concert Saturday there was a party. The next weekend I saw balloons everywhere. I just didn't know what they were there for. It turned out that you put laughing gas in the balloon and sold it. Andy told me what he had done. I saw that as an enterprising idea but had never heard of anyone doing that. He knew his drugs.

We were so good together people would study us and see the happiness and love. We didn't have much of a sex life. He may have turned out to be the best I ever had, but he started out slow. He really started out slow. Eventually, not too long into the relationship, I asked him to help me stop drinking and he said he would. I had asked two other people prior to asking him and they said, "No". One was in AA (Alcoholic Anonymous). I'm glad they said no. I wish I had known an attachment would be formed with the person that helped you stop drinking. I formed a very real attachment to Chief when four months later I gave his nephew and his friend a beer. I had two beers I gave away and one kept one so I could say I had one if I wanted to be stupid and drink it. Chief always had marijuana and we smoked a lot of it all the time. The marijuana helped me stop drinking along with a desire to be a better person for my children. I needed my life back. I didn't want to drink beer from morning until I practically passed out. I spent a lot of money on beer.

I went with Andy to pick up quarter pounds of marijuana. He told me he was getting it from a dead policeman's son and there was no way we would get caught. I would go into the mall and when I came out the transaction would have been made.

He had a selected clientele of doctors, lawyers. He had a system. He was good. We also went out to eat at a restaurant downtown three or four times a week on the way home from the mall meeting. It cost about one hundred dollars to eat there, especially when you're buying beer, too. And he didn't like cigarettes and I smoked them.

Since I did smoke cigarettes he didn't kiss me. He said it tasted like kissing an ashtray and even though we were so much in love he wouldn't kiss me or have sex with me. He made me feel loved. We saw each other almost everyday. We had one collect phone call when I called him that ran up to thirty dollars.

We broke up when he told me he might get busted and we shouldn't see each other for six months. I broke up with him. One of my friends was there and I had cramps. I had the things he had left at my house all packed and together. He didn't want to break up. I didn't want to get in any trouble so I made him leave. He says he cried and he did cry sometimes. He was capable of crying at the drop of a hat or he didn't really cry. I did see him cry at other times.

We resumed seeing each other six months later. We started spending Friday, Saturday, Sunday and most of the day Monday at the lake again. One weekend Jim and Jill came to stay in the lake house.

Andy was calling Jill baby and Hon and I asked her husband how I was supposed to know who Andy was talking to. Jim said I don't know and looked bewildered. He knew something was up with those two. There were two beds in the room, they slept in one and Chief and I slept in the other. I thought it was weird considering there was another whole bedroom downstairs. I got up with Jill and the baby the next morning. I didn't sleep very well but I still couldn't tell you if Andy and Jill had a midnight roll in the hay. Maybe that's why they didn't sleep in the other bedroom. Maybe they needed the bed for their whatever they were doing.

We couldn't break up soon enough for Jill. She actually told me on Chief's birthday that if something happened to Jim, Chief would marry her and take care of her and her baby. It says a brother should marry a widowed sister in law. I couldn't imagine the audacity it took for her to tell me this with her husband a short way away from her. She was sitting in a chair and Andy was sitting in a chair next to her. I think it was Chief's baby. He called himself Uncle RARA. DADA. Jim and Jill had been married twenty years and had no children. Then Chief moved in with them after he faked the extremely high blood pressure. He has animal magnetism. I know she got confused.

He also got them addicted to cocaine and practically ruined them financially. I told them I would not go on the Jerry Springer show when Jill told me of her plan in front of Chief and her husband. Chief and I broke up about a week later. Jill had both her men back. I didn't want any legal problems as a result of our dating so I was able to sit and wait six months. I went out and did what I wanted to do. I didn't drink anymore.

Jill didn't scare me, but, she was very possessive of Chief. She couldn't stop him from seeing me though. She was always uncomfortable when I was around. The baby grew bigger and I talked and played with her when we went to their house. Jill didn't have much to say to me. She was polite and that was the extent of our relationship. Six months later I called Andy at his brother's house. I left a message for him to call me and he did. We broke up and got back together about four times during our love affair. The whole time I knew I loved him and he loved me.

Chapter 12

I HAD TO have a hysterectomy. I had met a sober man, a real man, at the craziest bar in town. I didn't drink anymore. I went to watch the patron's get drunk and act stupid. Andy and I were broken up and had been for over a year. I went in the bar on March 16, 2001 and he was there. He told me he had seen me five years earlier when I went in with my mother after we visited my Great Aunt in the hospital. She was dyeing.

We got married in Gatlinburg at a small wedding chapel. I wore a summer dress, sleeveless, green with white flowers in the pattern. We went to a time share presentation to get fifty dollars we used to spend the night. We got pictures developed on the way home. Our wedding night dinner was Wendy's. We stayed in the oldest hotel in the area so the furnishings were old and primitive. We had a balcony. We had a chest with Diet Coke in it. I can't do anything without a Diet Coke in my hand.

I had a hysterectomy about a month later. I had a complication. I got a blood clot in my right lung. The hospital put me on the "waiting to die" floor and the nurses always stuck their heads in before they came in. I was in the room with another older woman. I don't know what was wrong with her. I felt so bad. My Daddy called and all I could say was I feeling too bad to talk. I hung up. I literally felt too bad to talk. I was in shock, I couldn't believe that I could bleed out and die any minute. I was in the hospital from Sunday until Friday. I was miserable. I was still hurting from the hysterectomy incision and I was uncomfortable. My husband came and saw me before work for a short time and after work for a short time. I was used to being in the hospital with someone with me twenty four hours a day. He just couldn't take off work. He had started his job in April and I had the hysterectomy in September. I had been in the hospital the whole week before also. I think the blood clot was a result of negligent care on the hospital's part. I wasn't ever out of bed.

I spent the next six months battling the blood clot. My husband took excellent care of me and if it weren't for him I probably would have died. He worked two jobs. I couldn't return to my job. I had a good job that paid very well. I was the business manager for an electrician.

My husband did everything that needed to be done. All I could do was sleep on the couch and wake up to smoke marijuana or eat. I had to go three times a week for blood to be drawn to make sure my blood wasn't too thin. I had one scare. They called and told me to get to the hospital immediately but their test was wrong.

Yes, I smoked marijuana while I had a blood clot in my lung. I believe God put all things on earth that we need and marijuana has wonderful medicinal effect. I don't smoke marijuana anymore.

That all happened after the first time I met Chief. I called him to tell him I was getting married and he didn't return my call in time. After I recovered my current husband and I were living in the trailer my Daddy had bought me for $2500. There is talk he bought it for me as my mother said. I was also told my step mother bought if for my mother. All I know is I paid the property taxes and when I left my mother sold it and made money.

Chapter 13

AFTER THE HYSTERECTOMY I was in menopause, I had to go to a cancer doctor for a screening to see if I could have hormone replacement therapy. It turned out I could. If I didn't have a patch I was a wreck.

Chief had a friend that lived about two miles from the trailer we lived in, our home. During this time Chief came back around during the day. He would tell me how much he loved me and all the things a girl wants to hear. He even shed real tears. He talked me into leaving my trailer and my husband. He had me on cocaine and meth and I didn't even know it. I am so nieve it pains me for believing the good in people. I still believe there is good in people.

Chapter 14

C HIEF AND I left with a suitcase of my clothes on a Friday, payday Friday to tell the truth. We had my husband's whole check plus my check. I thought we would have money for groceries. What we had was money for Chief to put up his arm or nose or both. They always gave me cut. They didn't even know I knew I was smoking baking soda or snorting Vitamin B12. They were fiends and that I wasn't doing the actual drug or how it felt was a God sent blessing for me.

I didn't know it but he was using a needle again. He had always told me to the day the last time he used a needle and it had been over six years. He started again when my mother and sister were both in the hospital. The hospital the ambulance had taken my mother to be a six bed facility. The nurses were pretending to give her pain medication. They were actually shooting up with her pain medicine. Andy saw them and told me. I never would have known. That's when he started with the needle again. He got into the drug storage and stole two vials of ninety nine percent cocaine and some needles. After that he stayed at my sister's house and didn't go back to the hospital. The day of my mother's surgery he went home. He was back on the needle and I didn't know anything about it.

When the day came that we were to begin our life together we stopped at the Bait Store that I frequented. Chief went in and bought some oil and went to the restroom. The next thing I know my husband is standing behind me. I called out for Andy and he came running my husband stumbled backwards on the uneven floor. The cashier and sort of friend asked me if she should call the police. I told her no. We walked out, he got in the van and I got in my car. We jumped straight to the interstate in rush hour traffic and swerved in and out and went fast until my husband gave up the chase. I hurt him, but in a way he understood.

Chief and I met his good old friend and got some cocaine for our first evening together. Dewey's girlfriend was cutting it with plaster so that was a problem. Not for them but for me. I wasn't doing that stupid shit. I did go to a house that a "band" lived in and do some coke and I felt great. This was the only time I had knowingly did cocaine and felt good. God protected me by putting me with people who had no conscience and bad habits when it came to drugs. I count myself very lucky.

For the first year life was easy. It was filled with love. Chief couldn't do enough for me. We made love sometimes for 28 hours. The mattress would slide off the bed and that didn't stop us. The whole mountain heard about me living with the Chief.

I was taking my medication for depression and anxiety so I slept every night. Chief would go places and leave me alone in the house. I didn't know because I was asleep. I don't think he ever slept.

I was so happy. I was in love and he was in love with me. It took three months to get my furniture, etc. moved to the mountain. Everything was off loaded to the "barn". It wasn't a barn so much as it was a building his mother used to throw parties when her husband was alive. It had a full kitchen and a bathroom.

After everything was unloaded Chief and I walked across the street to the house. We were holding hands and I was so happy. We talked about how we would never be apart again. I looked at the lake and I felt safe and secure with Chief. It took Chief another month for him to move my furniture into the house.

He decided it was time to put my things in the house when we came home one night. I suggested we check the barn. When we pulled up two guys were leaving. We went into the barn and there were space heaters on and it was summer. Someone was trying to burn down the barn. If we hadn't come back at just the right time I would have lost everything that night.

I replaced the 1970's with the things I owned. I took the house and made it mine. Chief took the knick knacks and everything that was his mothers and traded them for meth. We were doing meth non-stop. Every three or four days we slept. Chief had no intentions of getting a job or trying to support us legally. All he knew was drugs. I was blinded by my love for him. I felt safe with him. I felt happy and secure. I had never really expected anything to come of our relationship. Now we were living together. My birthday was in October and we celebrated. I bought a new outfit, we went to a couple of his old friends. We snorted a little coke. I didn't feel anything. Chief and his friend played the guitar. We talked. That was the first birthday I celebrated with him as his live in girlfriend. We had never discussed marriage and I was happy not being married to him. To me it didn't matter because we were soul mates and would be together until one of us died and that was all that mattered to me.

Chapter 15

H IS MOTHER COULDN'T afford to support us any more than she was already doing. She paid the electricity bill, the phone bill, the water bill, the taxes and insurance. We went for assitance in the form of food stamps. I got a lease from his mother that is on file in the state we were in. Chief got one hundred plus dollars a month. I qualified for ten dollars each month. My money made me have an income that didn't qualify except for ten dollars a month.

Chief dreamed of getting a disability check. There was really nothing wrong with him. He faked high blood pressure and said he had a back problem. I didn't see any evidence of a back problem but he sure liked to take pain pills.

When we needed food Chief would steal sometimes. Sometimes we went to the Salvation Army and got "food boxes". We got a can of horsemeat dog food out of one box. I kept it on with the date we received it and put it on display. To me it represented a time that we struggled and I just knew things would get better. I was deluded enough to think Chief would work and things would get better for us. I talked to him about going to work as a life insurance agent again. He said that would cause us problems. I don't know what I was thinking. I was so much in love and he professed his love for me all the time.

Andy was actually in the bed most nights during the first year. If not in the bed, in the chair beside me. During the cold, we kept a fire in the fireplace. The room was beautiful and huge. The fireplace was stone and it was beautiful, magnificent. Andy gathered box wood from the side of a lumber plant where they sawed and planed wood. The pieces burned fast, hot and had to be replaced about every thirty minutes. It would be out by morning.

About four thirty one morning Andy woke me up. He said it was an earthquake. The earth was moving. There were huge beams directly above the bed, on Andy's side of the bed. I looked and everything was moving. I said maybe the big tree in front was falling. No, it was an earthquake. When it stopped I rolled over and said "I better go back to sleep in case there are after shocks". And went to sleep. Randy couldn't sleep. Finally, about nine o'clock he woke me up. He had cooked. I had breakfast in bed a number of times. I thought he was so sweet. He was always physically appealing to me even if he was short, large, and bald headed. His eyes were so kind. I could see what I thought was his soul in his eyes.

I never had to cook. He told everyone I was a twentieth century fox and didn't have to cook. I did clean the house and wash the dishes. The only thing the lake house was missing was a dishwasher. It was such a small area there wasn't room for one.

After three months he wouldn't let me get my depression medication filled and I had started doing meth so the medication wouldn't have done me a lot of good. Everyone on that mountain, young or old, did meth. It was the biggest industry on the mountain. There were no employers in the area unless you went down the mountain and these people never left the mountain.

Chapter 16

THE HOLIDAYS, THANKSGIVING and Christmas were not observed by us. We did attend the family gatherings. We managed to actually make it off the frozen mountain and get down to somewhere it wasn't frozen.

The lake would freeze in motion. You could see the movement of the water but it was frozen. I loved watching the sun come up from the bay window. It was so cold and frozen yet people were still coming over. They would bring people and sometime meth and do it at our house.

The first Christmas was ok too. I think I got a present but I don't remember what Chief bought me. We managed to attend the family gathering again. We got presents there. His mother and sister and Jim and Jill bought us presents. We didn't buy any presents. He never even mentioned it. I guess that was because he was still getting money from his mother. She couldn't afford to give him twenty dollars every time she saw him. She did give me a lamp made out of a fishing reel and rod. I collected old lures and bobbers and hung them on the wall. I had a lizard that was just frozen in time. His eyes were open and everything but he was dead. I hung my Grandfathers fish. It was from Rock Mountain Lake. It really looked good in there. I loved it. My grandfather had taught me how to fish and I was the only one he would take fishing with him. He let me do everything but take a fish off the hook. He let me put worms and Catawba worms on the hook. Catawba worms look like lime marshmallows. He taught me how to put them on a line. He always had milk cartons full of brim. The fish he had mounted was a record setting rock bass. I don't know why Dewey would want to tear up something that was priceless to me. It really hurt my feelings.

The same day Chief slammed the door and broke the platter that went to my Great grandmother's china. I didn't have many pieces in the first place and he broke the platter I had hanging on the wall. I had given Sherry and Cheryl one of the small bowls because they were good friends to me. Sherry told me what she knew and Cheryl told me what she knew. They ran in a different group. I guess they didn't want to come while there was someone cooking.

One evening in the spring I got a call from Cheryl. She was locked in her house by her boyfriend that lives with her. Their house overlooked a huge bluff and you could see stars. The kitchen was perfect, one bathroom was perfect. That bathroom had a dresser with a sink sunk into it. The house was way out in the woods though. I told her I'd come and get her. I drove through the three rocks so big they built the road around them. I got to her gate and it was locked. She really was locked in. I was in the truck so I went around the gate going in and coming out. She came over and we drank some beer, etc. She was one the girls that asked me to help her get baptized. I told them what they needed to do in the meantime and that we would when they came to me not at four a.m. and wanted to be baptized. I could get a preacher to do it any day, but the middle of the night is a really hard sell. The preacher has obligations also. Once you bring someone to God they are yours to take care of. I have been unable to keep up with that but I keep them in my prayers.

They did come over and they criticized the house and told us what we were doing wrong in their opinion. I appreciated that because I did everything I could but when someone's sitting directly below the Lane Shaker Reproduction Limited Edition table with seven chairs, two of them armchairs, five were armless cooking meth I guess the chemicals penetrate the wood and the carpet, etc. I was sitting at that table painting rocks with the stereo on. My stereo. I bought it. Chief broke it and took it. He really loved me. I like sarcasm. I don't know how I could have been in love like that with someone who would take all my worldly belongings. That tells me that something is way wrong. I'm sure that he made me out to be crazy on drugs and doing all kinds of "Bad" things once I left for my life.

Everything I owned had sentimental value to me. Everything they took and stole and gave away like it was garbage was priceless to me. My grand mother's chair. My great Aunt's trunk. Everything. The things the kids made in school and Bible school. I still can't wrap my head around that all my things are gone, my autographed first run John Grisham book, My Clinton inaugural ball stuff, the sound track was gone. The letter opener was gone. Everything was gone. No matter how special it was to me. My great grandfather's chest of drawers or dresser. It was hand made. It had a marble top on part of it. You can see dresser's like I had in the Cartwright's house. It makes me physically ill that I lost all these things. That is why I tried like hell to be there long enough without any drama so I could make arrangements to take my stuff with me when I went. No such luck. I didn't sue because I was afraid of retaliation from Andy. I already know what he said about revenge being a dish best served cold. If my car ever blows up or I get a snake for a present for the rest of my life I will know who is responsible. I'm not afraid of him, I pray to God that all his associates, friends, family and him will stay outside a five mile radius of me at all times. God didn't let him kill me then so I figure I don't have anything to worry about now.

Dewey broke my lizard and my fish. One night we had a lot of men over and some cooking went on. One man told me to take a pill he gave me and that if the police came we would go to the mental hospital. I thought it was a strange thing to say to me. I felt uneasy, Dewey was acting scared. I told him Nut called and he was scared too. I told him that the DEA was crawling through nut's yard and he believed me. He was so stupid. He threw my CD's around like he didn't pay for them and he didn't pay for them. Not even after he destroyed one.

Dewey didn't know there actually were people out there. I saw the night vision goggles on the boat to prove it. I looked at the boat during the daytime and didn't see anything out of place. One night I saw people walk up from the lake and sit on the neighbors porch. I could see all of them. There were about eight. They stayed there for about an hour and left going toward the road. I never knew who they were.

Chief told me a story about how he jumped somebody in his mother's yard one night. He was all in black, and very terrifying he thought he was telling me. I wasn't so sure. Of course, you never see the man do the things he tells you he did.

I have the misfortune of knowing it to be a fact. One night Chief and I went to my uncle's house. It turned out that Chief and my uncle had met in a hotel room and cocaine and guns and closets and my uncle being naked were involved. They went out on the carport and resolved everything I guess before I knew there was a problem. I knew my uncle looked scared but I knew he was a runner himself so I thought he had to be as tough as Chief. No, from the way he acted Chief had him down a couple of notches. My Uncle asked me if I was afraid of Chief and told him No, he helped me stop drinking.' I invited him over but he called up with some story about his wife thinking I was flirting with him and he couldn't come. I think it went more like "I'm afraid to come over there."

Dewey was a consistent problem with us. He came and stayed. One day Randy and Dewey had this great idea to go get a couch and take a victrola to sell. They had me get dressed up as I was the one who was supposed to make the deal. We ended up at some of Dewey's "friends". They played pool, there were no other girls there and we stayed until the sun came up. I don't know what kind of drugs they were doing. I sat in the truck a lot. Andy was out there some but they were doing something in that house that Dewey didn't want to stop doing. I had to sit on the arm of the couch. Dewey had gotten a van for this field trip.

Chief thought it was alright. His brother had said you can get the couch, it's in our way. It turned out I was at Kroger the next morning at seven am getting donuts and soda with Randy's food stamp card. That was embarrassing. We drove around that night looking for crack cocaine. It was like they'd both gone crazy and had to have some crack. They got a guy in the truck with me in the back. They didn't know him and I certainly didn't. Dewey was driving crazy. He went down one way streets the wrong way, ran traffic lights and stop signs. We drove along like that four about four hours. I was sick at my stomach to think that we could and most likely would get pulled over and go to jail. Thank God that's about all that didn't happen that trip.

They finally decided they needed to get home and it was time to sell the things they had gathered up. They sent me in one place and they said they weren't interested without even looking at what we had. I know how I looked. I looked like I'd just spent the day and night with two crazy people and Dewey was the craziest. He is the only one that can get Chief doing dangerous things. I don't know. Chief decided he would sell what we had in the truck for enough money to get gas and some cocaine on the way home at a second hand store for about two hundred and fifty dollars. Joyce wanted to press charges against us, but Jeff was still afraid to tell her the truth. The neighbors had seen all three of us. At this time Chief was good enough to admit that I had nothing to do with the plan or the removing of the furniture. I knew his mother would want that Victrola and I couldn't believe she left it in the house with Randy. He'll sell your soul without telling you if you let him. He won't give you any of the credit after you make everything alright for him. The only thing is you don't want a mad Jill, especially Andy, so you just don't tell her everything.

We were finally on the interstate. Andy had gotten some amount of money. He didn't tell me about the money he had or didn't have. He just did what he did. I was in the back seat on the way home. Without the couch and the victrola the back seat would go up. I was much more comfortable. The ride back took about three hours. Then we had to stop at someone's house and they went in. I think they were trying to get coke. I guess they needed some more crack. I never smoked crack, I smoked baking soda. I knew, but they didn't know I knew. People on drugs are really easy to fool or mess with. They had the "gotta have some more of that stuff" blues, not me.

We went with Dewey over to this house this guy had bought for a rental property and he bought it furnished. We picked out all kinds of junk and took it home with us. Some of it was good junk. That guy asked me what I was doing with Chief. Now I think I see why he asked me that question. At the time I was indigent. Don't criticize the love of my life was exactly how I felt about that guy. He thought he was all that. He was also married.

I gathered so much stuff from so many places. I had a chicken suitcase even. I talked another guy named Dewey out of his chicken suitcase and displayed it proudly in the lake house. This Dewey was born and raised on the mountain. He was related to the Sheriff. He was actually a gentleman towards me every time I saw him at first he didn't understand why I wanted that chicken suitcase so bad. Finally he gave it to me. I found a piece of glass to lay on the top and used for display next to the table where I sat and painted, read the Bible, worked on the business plans for "Rocks In My Head". I did all kinds of things at that table.

The chicken suitcase, as I called it, was made from twigs that were wired together. It was used to transport chickens to fights.

Chief would get money from his mother or his brother. His brother paid the co-pay for my hormone patches. Without the patch I was a mess. The hysterectomy had put me in menopause in a big, bad way. Without the replacement hormones I would cry, be very ill, although I didn't act ill toward Chief. I loved him too much for that. I don't like to fight or act badly.

Chief knew lots of people on the mountain. In the time we had been apart he had gotten to know all the people on that mountain. We frequently had people stopping by to see Chief and the new girl on the mountain. There was a lot of curiosity about me.

It would be after my second birthday, before all the girls. There was one girl during the first year that caused me some grief. She came with two other girls and a bunch of guys. They came over to party at our house. This one particular girl was tired or something because Chief gave her one of my Xanax. Then he got a lap throw off the back of a chair and pulled it up over her all comfy. I was sitting at table and I went into shock. I was so hurt. I had never see Chief treat anyone like he treated me. The guys saw my face and left. They could see the hurt and the pain. I was sitting at my table watching the whole time. After all the guy left Chief went upstairs to the master and sat all night. I went into the room to get my makeup and Chief was sitting in a chair. He realized how hurt I was so he got away from that girl. I played with the girls that were awake. At one point it got so weird I gave them makeovers. They looked good with make up on.

The object of Chief's misdirected affection woke up about eight o'clock in the morning. I suggested we go to the store and get some soda and something to eat. I made her pay when we got there. We went by Dewey's house to see if he had any meth. He didn't. He had to cook more. I was glad he didn't have more. I didn't want that dumb girl in the house all day. I certainly didn't want to see him with her.

I told the dumb girl that if she could get Andy she could have him. He would love to have her and her kids all up in his house. She thought I was serious. She was telling me all about what time she would be there that evening. The only thing she didn't tell me were the kids names. You could see in her eyes that she had found her home.

She must have been warned because she didn't come back that evening and I only saw her when I was at Dewey's.

Chief always had someone to party with. All kinds of guys came around from on top of the mountain.

Dewey, his high school friend, learned about needles from Chief. Dewey also almost had to have his arms amputated. Dewey no longer had affection for the needle but he loved to smoke crack cocaine and snort cocaine. He and his girlfriend came over one morning with all kinds of cocaine looking for a good place to party. We were it. We partied two and a half days. I had a great time but I still ended up with a lot of cut. Chief invited a couple from the mountain over for a little while during our coke party. They did some with us and Dewey did his flash dance. I played along with him. He put a big pile of cut on the table and we pretended it was coke and snorted it and scraped it off the table onto the floor. While I was with Randy I had no qualms about asking these people for what I saw that they had that I wanted. They usually gave it to me.

When we weren't out socializing we watched television. Some days I felt so bad I laid in bed for days. Randy would sit in a rocking chair with his feet on the bed. I was content. I would sleep on and off. He made me ice cream cones. He cooked for me. He woke me up when he missed me. I think at that time he did love me. He told me one afternoon that if he started being meant I should go get in the closet and stay. He didn't want to hurt me.

His brother was always giving him money or buying things and giving them to us. He had his brother "help" him move the washer and dryer and hook it up. We had been going to his brother's house and washing clothes. It was winter and the lake was frozen in motion it was so cold. We took showers at his brother's house also. Sometimes they fed us. Looking back I can see that being Bipolar was the only thing that kept me from seeing the reality of my life with Randy.

I met a girl that was Bipolar. Everyone called her crazy Connie. A common misconception about Bipolar. Being Bipolar doesn't mean you are crazy. There are various degrees of Bipolar. Medication works.

Chapter 17

CONNIE HAD A cabin on the lake. At that spot the lake was small and her view wasn't so good. Her cabin was small. She had bought it with a five dollar down payment. Her parents helped her keep the cabin. I heard lots of rumors about her. It bothered me that everyone called her Crazy Connie but I was guilty of using that nickname for her also.

I don't know what happened to her. One day she was there and then she was gone. I had considered her a friend. We "played" together. We did meth and played cards.

After Connie left I had Brenda, Cheryl and Sherrie for "friends". They were the only three girls on that mountain that didn't flirt with Randy in front of me or throw themselves shamelessly at him. I wasn't jealous. I was so sure of Chief's love for me. I was positive no one could take him from me because he loved me.

That didn't stop them from trying. Any girl that showed up and flirted with him in front of me I kept an eye on. I would tell them "If you can get him, you can have him." I was so secure in our love that I just knew he wouldn't be interested in any of them.

Chapter 18

CHIEF WAS JEALOUS of the guys that came and talked to me. All they did was talk. If he caught one of them staring at me he would tell them "I know she's pretty, that's why she's here." If they talked or tried to even look like they were flirting he had them arrested. One guy in particular got pulled over on his way home from our house. I still didn't actually believe he was a DEA Agent.

I started to notice odd things in the house. There was someone in the attic. The house had cameras in the ceiling and recording devices. Andy told me the house was wired for sound and pictures. Anything, including going to the restroom, someone was monitoring. Andy would look at me every time he heard the noise coming from the attic. At night I saw night vision goggles. Someone was out there looking. He told me I was intel. People would tell me anything. All I had to do was ask one little question and then listen. I would tell him whatever they told me.

I found a "Police In Training" t-shirt in one of my drawers. I couldn't wear it and the next time l looked for it it was gone. I don't know how it got there and I don't know what happened to it. Chief had a DEA t-shirt. He had it hidden in a drawer. I found it when I was putting up clean clothes.

We would stay up all night frequently by ourselves. He would tell me stories of the things he had done to people that made him mad. He had wrapped up snakes like Christmas presents. He could catch rattlesnakes. He sold them to church's that use the snake bite method to determine faith in their members when he was a kid. He told me he put candy bars in people's gas tanks and then watched them walk when their car blew up. He did it over and over to drive them crazy. He never told me who they were. He did tell me he liked to wait years until the person would never even think he had done anything.

He told me about the years he lived in California. He made me laugh so hard I wet my pants literally. I had never seen this side of him. I don't think he talked to anyone like he did me. He told me all kinds of stories. He was a train engineer. I deduced that when he began his tale of being a train engineer was code for look at this situation. Start the cameras and action. He told me he had gotten arrested for writing prescriptions. He had been given probation and was required to work with the DEA doing busts on people for three years. He also told me that he had developed the codes the DEA uses now. He told me he was at MIT in a think at tank. The bad thing about this is I believe he could have been. I believed anything he said. I love him. I thought he loved me. He did love me until he got so bad on drugs and started mixing meth with prescription drugs he was shooting up.

Chapter 19

DEWEY AND HIS girlfriend got arrested with cocaine on their way to a concert. Dewey and his girlfriend had broken up and he had no where to stay so Chief let him stay in the guest room. Dewey was an idiot and was always doing something aggravating. Chief introduced Dewey to meth. It was cheaper than cocaine and had it's own merits in their opinion.

Dewey's girlfriend and I got along good. The first night I was with Randy she asked me for a clean shirt and I gave her one. It wasn't long before Dewey's girlfriend started showing up and threatening us. She wanted someone else in trouble with her. She was hooked on crack cocaine. Dewey got back together with her sort of. They didn't live together anymore but they were together.

After they got arrested Chief was afraid they would tell on him. To get on their good side Chief took six hundred dollars from me and bought cocaine. They were going to do crack. Crack is what you get when you put baking soda and cocaine in a spoon and heat it with a lighter. It hardens and turns yellow.

When Chief and Dewey got back with the coke they got excited. I knew they were giving me baking soda so I sat down to watch them. They insisted I smoke some too, not knowing that I knew they were giving me baking soda. I'm thankful they didn't give me the real stuff. I had prayed daily not to get addicted to anything. God was good to me and I didn't get addicted to anything except Andy.

Andy didn't take the garbage off the mountain for the whole winter. He stacked it in the back of a truck that didn't run and sat under the carport. Dogs and all kinds of animals got into the trash and strewed it everywhere. In March, I got out there and cleaned it all up. I found syringes in the yard. Everyone used needles on the mountain except me. Chief told people I didn't do that stupid shit. He was proud of that fact. I was supposed to be helping him get off the stuff. I don't know how I was supposed to keep him from doing whatever he wanted.

After I picked up all the garbage I took a shower. I made a comment that the water was cold. I was standing in the shower. He came in the bathroom, turned the hot water all the way on and I jumped back to keep from getting burned. When I did I fell on the metal track right onto my lower spine. I believe that is why I have such serious back problems now. I fell or was pushed, pulled and thrown away by Chief.

I did get him once. He wanted me to sit in the loveseat for the first time in ages. I sat down, well first I took the Owl killing rock and put it up, then I sat down with my legs in front of me just in case. He had the smirk like he was going to hit me and he had been hitting me a lot of the time. I kicked him softly with my Harley boots on and he flipped me over head first onto the floor. I cracked a rib. I don't know why he wanted me to sit down. He was with other women, not me. He hadn't touched me in a while.

Chapter 20

FOR ME, BEING Bipolar means that my thoughts never stopped. I made bad decisions. I was depressed for months at a time. My mother had told me she thought I was Bipolar but I didn't see it at the time. She also told me I had been abducted by aliens so I took everything she said with a grain of salt. I didn't want my mother to be right. I now know that my mother is Bipolar also. I've seen her Bipolar behavior. That's the thing about being Bipolar, you don't see yourself and what you're doing.

When I first got to the mountain there was talk that I was a cop. It never occurred to any of them that Chief might be a cop. He had told me he was a DEA Agent and I believed him.

The people on the mountain were so curious about me. I had one girl say to me "So I hear you come from money." I didn't say anything and changed the subject. Dewey and his girlfriend were visiting. I was causing quite a commotion on the mountain. People were so curious they had to come see me for themselves.

A couple of girls, Sherry and Cheryl liked me I thought. I know everyone talked about me. They were curious to see the girl that lived with Chief. Everyone was afraid of Chief. Everyone but me. In my wildest dreams I never thought he would hurt me in any way.

I always had my bible and word had gotten out the I was a believer in God, someone these people were all confused about. I doubt there were any that had ever been to real church. There was a rock church that was open twenty four hours a day, seven days a week. Everybody had been there but, it was empty except for the dead man buried in the inside wall. It was just a place to go and look for the mountain people.

I had the Prayer of Jabez written on the bathroom mirror. Everyone that went to the bathroom read the prayer and prayed in their own way. It was comforting to me.

Mountain people are different. I didn't think anything about that until I got to the mountain and started meeting these people. All the times at the lake all those years and we had never seen anyone there except a girl after Randy when we first started dating. Joyce and Jeff and one of Randy's cousins and his wife stopped by. No one else until I'd been living there for quite some time, word got out and everyone flocked around to look to see who lived with the meanest man that had the prettiest house on the mountain on the lake and they thought he was rich.

Chapter 21

H E WASN'T RICH. He tried selling them marijuana but everyone on Meth doesn't want to buy or smoke marijuana so Andy decided to go into the Meth business himself and take over the business on the mountain. There were two other cookers and they were loosing business fast and not liking it.

He decided since no one wanted marijuana he would go into the meth business. He began having "cooks" make meth in the kitchen. Sometimes he made me go with him to round up the ingredients that go into meth. Those were dangerous times. I was never afraid. I trusted him. He did tell me he was a DEA Agent. I thought nothing would ever happen to us.

Things got tense on the mountain. The two main suppliers on the mountain were loosing business. There was some ill will toward Andy but everybody knew they couldn't stop him.

We went to one of their houses, Nuts and there were all kinds of people there. About ten I guess, I didn't count. I was telling jokes and told everyone in the room that Nut was selling Nut Cut, not meth and the city should be giving him a bonus for keeping everyone regular with the baby laxative they cut it with and energetic with the B12 they cut it with. I shouldn't have said that in public.

Nut looked at me like he could kill me and Andy got me out of there quick. The next morning he went to talk to Nut to make sure Nut wasn't going to retaliate. I had made a joke that I had made many times with Andy. I just never told it to the audience in his house buying the stuff before and I couldn't believe I said it at the worst possible moment for Nut. I really liked Nut.

Nut's business suffered for a while but he forgave me. Nut and I had a good relationship. He gave me things from his house that I liked and I gave him things he liked. He was nice to me except for the one time he called me Barb, and told me to get out of his house. I hollered back at him "My name is not Barb and you don't holler at me and you can't kick me out of your house." He was shocked. No one talked to him like that. I did and I lived to tell about it. Nut was also in the pill business and Chief would sell him medicine—my medicine, trade it for meth and he would buy the stuff back at street prices. I never had my medication the two years I lived with him on that mountain.

The second summer was filled with meth. It was spring. A paramedic guy started coming to our house. One Sunday night Chief was cooking for me and I put on a shirt and went downstairs. The kitchen door window was glass with a sheer curtain on it.

He was smoking a cigarette and standing on the carport looking in at us. Andy opened the doors and asked him what he needed. Andy didn't like him standing there looking at me in my underwear.

I don't remember his name, but he was sandy blonde. About six feet two inches and he had a very pleasant face. I liked him and Chief acted like he liked him. He would come by and smoke meth or marijuana with us.

One night he showed up. We were sitting at the table inside the bay window with the lights on. The porch lights were on and the dock lights were on. It was about ten thirty p.m. when two jet ski's came roaring down the lake. They pulled up beside one another facing the house and looking in basically. We didn't get scared, we just watched them. I had told Andy that I had dreamed this exact incident, and I had. I have dreams or wake up knowing something is going to happen. It happened. Did Andy set it up? I don't know, but that would have fit in with his DEA story very well.

I felt like I was in a movie. I didn't usually walk around with a knife on my belt. There was about a month that I thought it was warm enough for shorts. The rest of the time I wore jeans and Harley boots. I loved my Harley boots. They kept me from getting bit by a snake while I looked for rocks across at the stream in front of the barn. It was wooded but the neighbors had used it to keep their horses. The trails they used were clean. I loved walking back through there. One day I was cleaning off the rock that looked like the rock under the house. It had leaves and pine straw on it and I brushed it off with a stick. I stood on the rock and looked around. I looked down at the rock and saw it was oblong shaped. It was about four feet off the ground because it sat on other rocks. It was about four feet from the stream. I realized suddenly that there was an Indian buried under the rocks I was standing on. Then I realized there was an Indian buried under the rock under the house in the secret room. The dirt and the rock, just like the one across the street at the creek, had not been disturbed.

Andy and I were in the master bedroom one afternoon. I was in bed watching television and he was sitting in a rocker with his feet up on the bed watching television. I heard kids laughing right outside the French doors on the other side of the room. It didn't last long. Randy looked at me, I looked at him. I wondered out loud if there were children there. I knew there weren't. There were about six houses on the road. Andy said he had heard them before. The spirit of the Owl tribe had not been erased from this spot. It was beautiful and all the evidence pointed to this land being uninhabited until the house was built.

Andy's mother, Hortence, had inherited the house from her second husband. She had divorced Andy's dad and I could see why. She had remarried. He happened to own a company that made a significant amount of money. She sold the neighbor on the left part of the land across the street. She used the money to pay the taxes on the house.

Our house had a lot in between it and another house on both sides. It was a quite peaceful area before Chief moved in.

Chapter 22

C HIEF WOULD TAKE my medication away from me and sell it and "eat" it. If I was lucky I got a couple. He alienated me from my family, let my driver's license expire and not get it renewed and my car be repo. I was blinded by love and never saw he was destroying me. I thought the first year was a good year. We would make love for twenty eight hours at a time. The mattress would slide off the bed and we didn't stop. We were like a puzzle that fit perfectly. He had lost weight on the "Jenny Crank "diet and he looked good. His penis seemed bigger too since he didn't have the stomach to contend with.

He had shot himself in the leg about the same time I had the blood clot. Some girl that he had brought home with him told him someone was outside. He took a loaded gun and held it down to the side of his leg and it miss fired. He pulled the gun down on the girl and scared her to death. Then he got hemostats and pulled the hot bullet out. He went and finished a plumbing job at a church he had been working on. The backhoe filled with blood. He finished, got inspected and went home. He told that girl when he got back she better not be there. She robbed him and left.

His best friend, I guess as far as Chief had friends, he had people he manipulated mostly. He was the master. Nut came running on a motorcycle in the cold through the woods. Nut was in another state. We were about a mile from the state line.

Nut came running with a girl whose mother was a nurse. She told them to take him to the hospital. He didn't go. The friends stayed and kept an eye on him fed him pain pills. Probably booze too. He got better. That is when he decided he wanted me desperately. He began his pursuit and he got me. I was stupid to believe him but I thought it was "true love", he was my soul mate. We told each other we loved each other so much we hated each other. We could talk to each other about different topics at the same time and know what each other was talking about. Our sex life was the best I ever had.

While Chief was recovering from his gunshot wound he had a guy that moved in on him. When Chief was through using him, he still wouldn't leave. Chief left the house for three days and locked that guy in the house. When he finally came home that guy ran out and didn't come back for a while.

I respected the house and took good care of it. I cleaned things that hadn't been cleaned in years. It was a beautiful place and I knew I was blessed to be living in such a place.

Chapter 23

THE SECOND YEAR on my birthday he had a cooker for meth and woke me up on my birthday, after putting me to sleep literally, about 10:00 p.m. I had been asleep all but two hours of my birthday because Chief had given me something to knock me out.

There was a girl there that wanted Andy—Kim—and there was a guy there that wanted Kim. They were having a spoon party. I called it a spoon party because they used a big serving spoon and liquefied the meth and shot up. I swallowed the meth wrapped in paper. Smoking it was a messy thing to do. The glass pipe would turn black and have to be cleaned. I would get black all over my hands, sometimes on my face. Swallowing it was just easier.

Kim moved into the barn. She stored what she had left in the barn. Andy had had a relationship with her or had sex with her before we got together and I moved there. She wasn't taking the fact that I was there very well. She was attractive and flirted with Andy shamelessly. I wasn't happy they were there. There was a huge difference in my birthday the year before and this birthday. It was the beginning of the second year.

My second birthday I got a battery powered plastic rose. Cheap and stupid. That was all he said he could afford. A girl after my man and a man I didn't want to spend my birthday with. I don't remember much else, I was pissed and Chief was acting badly and I didn't know what to do about his bad behavior. The spoon party lasted all night. My birthday was ruined. There was no one to call to talk some sense into him. He was on drugs I didn't even know he was on.

Chapter 24

THE SECOND YEAR life consisted of a cook being in the house all the time. He had decided we needed a live in cook. Kim was in the barn and wouldn't leave. Andy was going over there and visiting with her. I think he was having sex with her. The way she acted I was sure of it.

Word got out I was going to beat her ass. I've never been in a fight and I don't think ladies should fight. I was just going to punch her once in the nose with my right hand ring. The last time I saw her she didn't get out of her car for very long because I walked out to meet her with my ring finger right hand ready to punch her square in the nose. I'd had enough of her.

Andy had begun to be violent with me. I ignored his advice to hide in the closet. I was sitting at the table and he took a big knife and stabbed my table to scare me and hurt me. His huge knife was sticking straight up out of my table. I was seeing red I was so mad. I took a rock and really scratched it. It was supposed to be distressed anyway. It looked old. It was a Lane Shaker Reproduction limited item. I paid $3000 for it and I loved it from the very first time I saw it. I don't know who has it now.

Chapter 25

THE SECOND YEAR I witnessed my first "spoon party". Andy had a hugs spoon from the kitchen filled with meth ready to be shot up. The girl that had her stuff across the street in the barn with the kitchen, bathroom and fire pit was there. One of the guys that "cooked" was there. Chief looked so happy to be having a spoon party. I though at that time he might like me better if I joined in the spoon party. I didn't say anything at the time. I wanted my first time to be just between me and Andy. The first time came about two weeks later. I told him what I wanted to do and he did it to me. I could never do that to myself. I didn't feel much of anything. I didn't realize that was using mostly water. I also didn't realize this would take me off the pedestal he had put me on for not shooting up. That was the second year. He did that to me about twenty five times and the last time is when I left with the police. He gave me a shot that was intended for him. He had never been so cold to me. He just shot me in the arm and went in the bathroom to shoot up.

The second year I studied the mountain. The owl Indians were the last inhabitants. I started collecting rocks in a wheelbarrow and washing them off, scrubbing them with a toothbrush. Sometimes I had to let them soak. I was having such a good time and learning at the same time. I found all sorts, colors and shapes. of rocks.

I found rocks that were cats, birds in flight, fish, roses, dogs, alligators. I started painting the rocks. It was like coloring in a coloring book. I was keeping an inventory because I had decided to open a non-profit organization to help these people on the mountain with no future and pasts that were unbelievable. I had a rock that was of a white man on fire. One had twelve species of beings, human, aliens, women, and men. They were in a group picture like they were at a meeting. I discovered that if you turn a rock one way it is a human, the opposite way were animals. Turn it again and there was evil, the opposite were angels, good things.

I found rocks under the driveway that were blue and white. I washed them all and separated them according to size. There were three sizes. When I looked at them good I discovered that they were the exact same rocks, just in different sizes. I told people I was a "rockoligist". There is no such thing but as a "rockoligist" but no one knew that. Each person had there own specialty. The one thing they were really good at doing. I met a geologist. Word had spread all over the mountain.

I spent a lot of time studying rocks. I then decided to start a non-profit organization called "Rocks In My Head". My idea was to make the organization self sufficient with private donations for the rocks. I discovered arrow heads are not what people call arrow heads. Arrow heads have etched on them what could be killed with them. There were animals carved in the direction the arrow head should be used to kill what. I could go in the front yard and find arrow heads. I had three punch bowls full of them. After it rained it was like it had rained arrow heads. Just walk and pick them up. I found two rocks that were for killing by knocking on the head with the owl rocks. They had handles, were about two inches thick and were shaped like owls. The face was on both side and the detail was amazing.

I kept the small killing owl with me when Andy called me. I was ready for him to hit me or put the huge knife against my throat or my back. I had all the art from rocks in the great room displayed. Someone tried to destroy my art rocks with black paint. I got discouraged and asked God if I was doing the right thing, His will. My answer came in the form of a head rock. I went outside and started digging beside the driveway and I pulled the head rock out of the dirt and it left no hole. It was like the earth gave birth to that rock. The head rock had a face on each side. The carvings that made the faces were all smaller faces. It was blue and white and weighed about sixty pounds. I knew I was doing the right thing.

I rented one of the seven shops in the town. Tourists would have to drive right by and there were tours available that would bring people right in.

I was going to put a minimum donation on each rock. People could donate as much as they wanted but I placed a minimum donation on the art rocks. I made paper weights that were rocks that had no significant image on it and called them Paper Waits from the town I had the building in for souvenirs. I also made Witness Stones. They were flowers. The idea was to give one to someone you witnessed to.

I got one donation from the Shaman on the mountain. With him behind me people would help me. They brought me the most unusual rocks they had. I had a collection of ten. They were for display purposes like the head rock. I wrote my name on the bottom of the neck in green marker. I don't know who has it now. When I left I had to leave my rocks.

I never got to even set up the building. People gave me art and plants and things to decorate the building with. They would look for arrow heads and bring those to me. I had the support of all the people on the mountain. Andy did not support me until he got the idea he was going to run counterfeit money through the organization. He never let me go pick up the key to the building and after he got arrested and got me arrested on purpose the man that owned the building canceled my lease. He refunded my deposit. Andy told me he went to him and told him it was his fault I got arrested, but that didn't matter to the man that owned the building. When I finally had Kelly take me by the building there was a woman inside painting pictures. She had leased the building.

The people on the mountain were counting on me. They lived without electricity, without running water. They took baths in the creek. One friend, Debbie showed me the creek. Some people had no where to live. I was going to build dormitories without kitchens. I was going to drug test everyday and have a doctor to help with the detox. These people had been doing meth literally all their lives

Chapter 26

THE SECOND YEAR with the meth cookers was horrible. We were never alone. We had to go hide in the secret room in the basement several times. I would take my Bible with me and put it on my chest and cross my arms over. I would go to sleep immediately. I found that most of them didn't stay long. They were there on a trial basis. Some couldn't cook meth, they made a mess in the kitchen and ruined my microwave. They were potentially burning the house down, killing me from breathing the chemicals. I wasn't nervous. Andy was nervous although he told me he had guards along the road that would let him know if anyone was coming. By the time the worst one came Andy had the cooking done in the basement but not in the secret room. The worst one was Larry. He was a big boy and he was a felon. Chief made sure he didn't bother me he thought. Larry threatened to kill Andy if I told him that he had meth stashed up for himself. To get away from both of them when I cooked dinner that night I added a few ingredients to try to make them sick so I could get away. It didn't work. They knew. The house was wired for picture and sound and Andy knew when he walked in the house what I had done. Later that evening he knocked me out for the night. The next thing I know he is taking me to the doctor. He said he would have 240 hydroquinone and 240 bars of 2mg Xanax. He was going to take mine and they were going to kill me. Larry had a history of hurting women. He had tied his wife to a tree with barb wire and tortured her for eight hours. I could tell they were going to hurt me good by the way they were acting toward me and the words in the music he was playing.

I unplugged something in the back of the truck that I had never noticed, locked the door and drove off. Andy saw me unplug it and was standing beside the truck when I drove away. I kept seeing black DEA vehicles so I drove through backyards and down back roads. I hid the truck behind new construction and hid the keys and took my briefcase and my purse.

As I walked through the woods I had to put down my purse and briefcase. I had a corner baggy of what I'm sure Andy thought I would think was Meth. I knew it was poison and put it under a rock. I took off four rings and a watch he had took in on trade and threw them in case they had tracking devices. I came to a house and the lady and her child just drove off. I went to her porch and traded my timberland boots for hers and threw mine off the bluff. I didn't want dogs to track me. I found an ax and then I saw a barn. It was full of lie. I don't know what they did with that entire lie. I took the ax and went in the small house. It had been remodeled and was a good place for me to recuperate. I knew the people had to be home soon and they would help me. There was about a gallon of cold water in the refrigerator and nothing else. I took a toilet plunger and some razor blades and made myself a weapon. I slept there for two days. I never turned on the lights or anything at night and I always checked for the people to come home when I woke up. I needed help. I had what I had come to know as a DEA agent and a felon trying to kill me.

The little house had been totally remodeled. It was very beautiful and was furnished with new furniture, new comforters, pillows, everything was new. It was freshly painted. One bathroom was just off the bedroom.

The third day the water was gone and I was hungry. I went up to the big house. I walked around the outside, tried the front door and it was not locked. The big house was built just far enough away from a bluff in the mountain. The house had huge windows all the way around the room. It had two bedrooms upstairs. It was furnished beautifully. I choose the bedroom it looked like no one lived in very often. It had a wonderful bed, a great bathroom and a new computer. The bathroom was just off the bedroom. I never felt like taking a shower. I was just too tired. I found some Hershey bars and Dr. Pepper. I tried to eat some tuna but my stomach got upset. I put the rest in the refrigerator. Downstairs there was another kitchen. There were bunk beds all over in bedrooms. I don't know what that was all about. It looked brand new.

I could tell Christians lived there and I rested there three more days. I didn't know when the owners would come home and help me. I left a medication bottle in the small house with the toilet plunger, razor blade weapon I made when I fist got in the little house. I left a note about what happened under the downstairs kitchen sink. I guess it has never been found. The Sheriff said I didn't hurt anything and if I had wanted to I wouldn't have made the beds back up.

It had been five days and I didn't know any family phone numbers and couldn't call the police. I was in another state and I didn't know the county and I didn't know who Andy knew. I drank two beers, watched some race on the television and thought about my situation. First I was going to have to appear weak and messed up because Andy would unforgiving if I was all there. So I thought about the situation I was in. Then I decided I'd act like I had been poisoned. I wanted my belongings back so I decided to call Andy. I was feeling better. I had enough rest at least. I was scared that Andy would know I was faking.

I called the house the first time and Jim answered the phone. I waited a little while and called again. This time Andy answered the phone. I told him in a broken up speech pattern where I was and he said he would come get me. He says he looked for me but had been looking too far away. I had been about three miles from my own house. I had no idea where I was because I had taken back yards and woods to get there.

The truck had been found and was taken to an impound yard. Andy said his mother was mad I had stolen his truck. It was actually in her name. The truck was fine except for the face of the stereo was missing. I had decided it could be a GPS transmitter and took it off and threw it in the woods. Andy was convinced they stole it at the impound yard. The stereo didn't work at all if the front wasn't on.

I walked to a big rock in the fork of a road and waited. Neighbors that drove by and asked if I was alright kept calling him. He was screwing Amanda, married Amanda with two or three kids but a shameless flirt. And she always wore a dress. Easy access. She slept in our bed I bet. Finally after about two hours Randy came to get me. I pretended not to know anything but "I love Anny." I didn't pronounce his name or other words correctly. I pretended I was scared to death of Larry. Andy protected me and I protected myself from Andy. I didn't know what he would do to me if he knew I was not messed up in the head. He wanted to know if Larry had raped me. I managed to tell him about Larry threatening me and him.

Andy made me a ham sandwich and gave me four milligrams of Xanax. He put me to bed on the same sheets he had been screwing one of three whores. I went to sleep.

When I woke up I kept up the act. I was good. Andy believed I was messed up. I was hungry and got him to get me lots to eat. I had really had it now. How was I going to get my stuff and get away?

After a few days my daughter told Andy she wanted to see me before she called the police. I didn't tell her I was faking and ended up in the State Mental Hospital for the night. She didn't know I had insurance.

At this facility I was behind locked doors and gated. I was left on a bench for about an hour. Andy was outside. He looked in the door and looked genuinely concerned. He kept mouthing "I love you" through the glass. I kept sitting there being miserable. After about an hour I was taken to the actual hospital. They drew blood. I was put in the room with five other people on a cot up against the wall. The restroom was for men and women. I didn't want to go in there, especially at night. I had to urinate so I slid down my pants and urinated at the foot of the cot. I was in distress. I

We pulled into the police station and I sat up. The policeman asked me what was wrong and I told him everything that I was going through except the meth. I had been involved with a very mean man who was very good at being mean. He was supposed to be a DEA agent. He told me he was anyway. I thought, as he had said many times and many ways, that he loved me. When he didn't care I knew he would throw me out of the house or kill me, either way I was history for him. I had too many brushes with death at his hand and knew by the strength and grace of God I was still alive in the first place.

The policeman called a social worker. A nice, middle aged woman that listened to the whole story. How I was afraid of a man I, and everyone else, called Chief. How he would kill me after he tortured me. She took me to the hospital. I took off the wet clothes and was given paper clothes to wear. I was in a room lying on the exam table. I was tested and I dosed on and off the whole day. I was then told by the social worker I would be transferred to a mental institution.

Away I went, handcuffed, in the back seat of another police car in my paper clothes, my wet clothes in a bag. After an hour and a half ride, while I slept, we arrived at the mental institution. I was afraid and didn't really know what I was getting in to. I had no choice but, I didn't have to worry either. After a short wait in the lobby I was taken to the third floor. I was given dinner, even strawberry short cake. I was shown to a room, a bed and I slept there for two days. Each day a man drew my blood as they checked for drugs. I had marijuana, meth, Xanax, and hydrocodone in my system.

The Xanax was in my system because the night before I took four of them. There were about eight guys that I knew, there telling me they were taking me and Chief to the Witness Protection Program. These guys kept saying I was taking too much stuff. I wanted to take a few clothes, shoes, underwear and bras. I wanted to take a few pictures of my children and the corner of the quilt my great grandmother had made for me that she had inscribed with the date and my name and from her. I had planned to frame it. The quilt was beautiful and pink and I didn't know at that time how to care for it. My mother didn't think it was a big deal, to her it wasn't. I didn't realize how much it mattered until it was destroyed and the corner was all that was left. The guys disappeared by the next day and all that was left was a big scary memory. I woke to Chief and the needle and the meth. I was scared of him but could never, ever show fear. He had done what he had done many times before and injected me. He had always used water but the last time it was meth.

Chapter 27

WHEN MY SYSTEM was clean and I felt better I was still wearing the paper clothes. The girl in the room with me had my shoes on. I told one of the nurses and they made her give them back to me. She also took me to the closet that had clothes from patients that had left them. There were two pairs of overalls and a couple of shirts that would fit. I also saw the doctor. He put me on meds for anxiety and depression. My mother had somehow found out that I was there and had her talk with the Doctor. My mother was the first one to tell a Doctor that I was Bipolar. My daddy had learned of my commitment to the facility also and had his input with the Doctor. My session was just a technicality. The doctor was cold, noncommittal and didn't seem to care one way or the other.

My daddy came to see me after about five days. He was in the cafeteria when I got there. I was surprised to see him. I felt terrible about a phone call Randy had made me make. He made me call my Daddy and try to get twenty thousand dollars. I told my Daddy he would never have to worry about me again. My Daddy said "Don't call me again" and hung up.

After I ate lunch and my Daddy had some Jell-O he had to go home. I don't remember where he lived at the time, but I know he had made a long drive to check on me. He had my Aunt buy me some clothes and a little make up, underwear, bra's and socks. My Daddy has always been good to me and helped me any way he could financially. Our relationship was not so good. My Daddy told we would never get along because she was his wife and I was his daughter. I still can't call his house or know his address. I haven't seen him in years.

The facility on the other hand, was nice. The food was great and buffet style. After the last two years of hungry times it was great to have food, good food, as much as I wanted and a great selection. There was an inside swimming pool, a basketball court, workout room and facilities to wash clothes. Once again, God had taken great care of me and put me in a place so I could regroup. I could join society, sanity, and safety. I stayed for seventeen days. I stayed outside on the smoking porch most of the time. I was smoking again. I had quit. While in the hospital I met several men and women. One of the men wanted to be my boyfriend. We watched television together and I was confused. I still loved Randy and this man wanted me to be his girlfriend. I found out the next day he was there because he had played police officer with a light in his car. He pulled over a woman and raped her.

By this time I was taking Geodon (medication) for Bipolar and it knocked me out. I had expressed my concern to the doctor in writing that I didn't understand why I wasn't receiving a sedative. Geodon was fast acting and after I took it I could barely make it to my bed.

I got another roommate after a few days. She had checked herself in because of some marital problems. We went to the cafeteria and I saw all the keys lying on the counter. I picked them up and put them in my pocket. I took them to the room and hid them in the toilet. They found them eventually and I was banned from the cafeteria for about two days. The weekend doctor said I could go back to the cafeteria. I was glad because I didn't have any money. I had gotten five dollars from my Daddy and it didn't last long. I saved the plastic Diet Coke bottles and refilled them in the cafeteria. The last day I was there they said no one could do that anymore. Other people saw me doing it and started doing it too.

The head woman of the hospital on the floor I was on sold cigarettes. There were two men that were homeless that came to stay for a couple of days to eat and rest. They came twice while I was there. There was one man that thought he was from outer space. He tried to talk to me but I avoided him when I could and when I couldn't I just listened to his wild stories. After seventeen days I was released with a bus ticket to my cousin. The ride was four or five hours long. My cousin picked me up from the bus station. He took me to Wendy's and we got a hamburger. Then he took me to Walmart. He told me I could spend one hundred dollars. I got some paint, a CD by Jarule, some snack crackers and other miscellaneous things. While I was at my cousin's I was supposed to help him organize his papers and I cleaned house. I had to get everything situated before I could concentrate on the paperwork. I got it all sorted out and had started making file folders.

He took me to one of his rental properties on a Saturday and we spent the day painting the front of the house and making small adjustments to things that were half finished. I also went with him to his Husbands—he is gay—restaurant and cleared tables and washed dishes. They got slammed on a Sunday. He didn't ask me to do anything, I just saw what needed to be done and did it.

One day I called a taxi. I wanted to have my hair done. I had extensions put in. I had short hair and only one hairstylist could cut my hair the way I liked it. She was about one hundred miles away and I knew I wasn't going there any time soon.

The extensions cost me one hundred dollars plus I had to buy the hair. It was real human hair. My cousin was aggravated that I had called a cab and gone down to the hair stylist above his restaurant. I just needed something different. I liked the long hair but for some reason the front was still short so I had to wear a hair band to hide the difference in length. I still missed Randy and thought about us being together. All I could think of was the good times. I knew I couldn't be with him but I still wanted to.

Chapter 28

NO ONE SEEMED interested in what I had actually been through. I didn't feel comfortable enough to really talk about it to anyone so I didn't. No one knew how close I had come to death or how many times. No one knew the abuse, the suffering at the hand of Chief. No one asked and I couldn't talk about it yet. It was a time in my life that took years to sort through and get a grip on. I've never even had the courage to tell my Psychiatrist. I've told my mom a couple of incidents and I've told my husband a couple of incidents, but I didn't think anyone could believe the whole story of my time on the mountain.

Chapter 29

THE HOUSE WAS like going back to the seventies when you walked in. The mountain, the house, the lake. Everything was so beautiful. What's immaculately decorated are the well appointed and beautiful with a magnificent view of the lake from the bay window. The window was huge and you could see everything. In the Spring the drapes were the exact color of the leaves. It was a beautiful sight to behold. I loved to watch the sun set and rise. I loved to just sit and look at the window. I sat on the porch also. The walkway was rock. There were two huge rock fireplaces in the house. There was a boat dock. The Chief had built a secret room downstairs he attempted to grow marijuana. He attempted many illegal activities in this room. He hung people upside down to torture them. He was a very mean person when he wanted to be.

I can look back now and see that I did have some problems with the life experience. I can also see that God carried me many times.

Chapter 30

THE SECOND YEAR with the meth cookers was horrible. We were never alone. We had to go hide in the secret room in the basement several times. I would take my Bible with me and put it on my chest and cross my arms over. I would go to sleep immediately. I found that most of them didn't stay long. They were there on a trial basis. Some couldn't cook meth, they made a mess in the kitchen and ruined my microwave. They were potentially burning the house down, killing me from breathing the chemicals. I wasn't nervous. Andy was nervous although he told me he had guards along the road that would let him know if anyone was coming. By the time the worst one came Andy had the cooking done in the basement but not in the secret room. The worst one was Larry. He was a big boy and he was a felon. Chief made sure he didn't bother me he thought. Larry threatened to kill Andy if I told him that he had meth stashed up for himself. To get away from both of them when I cooked dinner that night I added a few ingredients to try to make them sick so I could get away. It didn't work. They knew. The house was wired for picture and sound and Andy knew when he walked in the house what I had done. Later that evening he knocked me out for the night. The next thing I know he is taking me to the doctor. He said he would have 240 hydroquinone and 240 bars of 2mg Xanax. He was going to take mine and they were going to kill me. Larry had a history of hurting women. He tied his wife to a tree with barb wire and tortured her for eight hours. I could tell they were going to hurt me good by the way they were acting toward me and the words in the music he was playing.

I unplugged something in the back of the truck that I had never noticed, locked the door and drove off. Andy saw me unplug it and was standing beside the truck when I drove away. I kept seeing black DEA vehicles so I drove through backyards and down back roads. I hid the truck behind new construction and hid the keys and took my briefcase and my purse.

As I walked through the woods I had to put down my purse and briefcase. I had a corner baggy of what I'm sure Andy thought I would think was Meth. I knew it was poison and put it under a rock. I took off four rings and a watch he had took in on trade and threw them in case they had tracking devices. I came to a house and the lady and her child just drove off. I went to her porch and traded my timberland boots for hers and threw mine off the bluff. I didn't want dogs to track me. I found an ax and then I saw a barn. It was full of lie. I don't know what they did with all that lie. I took the ax and went in the small house. It had been remodeled and was a good place for me to recuperate. I knew the people had to be home soon and they would help me. There was about a gallon of cold water in the refrigerator and nothing else. I took a toilet plunger and some razor blades and made myself a weapon. I slept there for two days. I never turned on the lights or anything at night and I always checked for the people to come home when I woke up. I needed help. I had what I had come to know as a DEA agent and a felon trying to kill me.

The little house had been totally remodeled. It was very beautiful and was furnished with new furniture, new comforters, pillows, everything was new. It was freshly painted. One bathroom was just off the bedroom.

The third day the water was gone and I was hungry. I went up to the big house. I walked around the outside, tried the front door and it was not locked. The big house was built just far enough away from a bluff in the mountain. The house had huge windows all the way around the room. It had two bedrooms upstairs. It was furnished beautifully. I choose the bedroom it looked like no one lived in very often. It had a wonderful bed, a great bathroom and a new computer. The bathroom was just off the bedroom. I never felt like taking a shower. I was just too tired. I found some Hershey bars and Dr. Pepper. I tried to eat some tuna but my stomach got upset. I put the rest in the refrigerator. Downstairs there was another kitchen. There were bunk beds all over in bedrooms. I don't know what that was all about. It looked brand new.

I could tell Christians lived there and I rested there three more days. I didn't know when the owners would come home and help me. I left a medication bottle in the small house with the toilet plunger, razor blade weapon I made when I fist got in the little house. I left a note about what happened under the downstairs kitchen sink. I guess it has never been found. The Sheriff said I didn't hurt anything and if I had wanted to I wouldn't have made the beds back up.

It had been five days and I didn't know any family phone numbers and couldn't call the police. I was in another state and I didn't know the county and I didn't know who Andy knew. I drank two beers, watched some race on the television and thought about my situation. First I was going to have to appear weak and messed up because Andy would unforgiving if I was all there. I thought about the situation I was in. Then I decided I'd act like I had been poisoned. I wanted my belongings back so I decided to call Andy. I was feeling better. I had enough rest at least. I was scared that Andy would know I was faking.

I called the house the first time and Jim answered the phone. I waited a little while and called again. This time Andy answered the phone. I told him in a broken up speech pattern where I was and he said he would come get me. He says he looked for me but had been looking too far away. I had been about three miles from my own house. I had no idea where I was because I had taken back yards and woods to get there.

The truck had been found and was taken to an impound yard. Andy said his mother was mad I had stolen his truck. It was actually in her name. The truck was fine except for the face of the stereo was missing. I had decided it could be a GPS transmitter and took it off and threw it in the woods. Andy was convinced they stole it at the impound yard. The stereo didn't work at all if the front wasn't on.

I walked to a big rock in the fork of a road and waited. Neighbors that drove by and asked if I was alright kept calling him. He was screwing Amanda, married Amanda with two or three kids but a shameless flirt. And she always wore a dress. Easy access. She slept in our bed I bet. Finally after about two hours Randy came to get me. I pretended not to know anything but "I love Anny." I didn't pronounce his name or other words correctly. I pretended I was scared to death of Larry. Andy protected me and I protected myself from Andy. I didn't know what he would do to me if he knew I was not messed up in the head. He wanted to know if Larry had raped me. I managed to tell him about Larry threatening me and him.

Andy made me a ham sandwich and gave me four milligrams of Xanax. He put me to bed on the same sheets he had been screwing one of three whores. I went to sleep.

When I woke up I kept up the act. I was good. Andy believed I was messed up. I was hungry and got him to get me lots to eat. I had really had it now. How was I going to get my stuff and get away?

After a few days my daughter told Andy she wanted to see me before she called the police. I didn't tell her I was faking and ended up in the State Mental Hospital for the night. She didn't know I had insurance.

At this facility I was behind locked doors and gated. I was left on a bench for about an hour. Andy was outside. He looked in the door and looked genuinely concerned. He kept mouthing "I love you" through the glass. I kept sitting there being miserable. After about an hour I was taken to the actual hospital. They drew blood. I was put in the room with five other people on a cot up against the wall. The restroom was for men and women. I didn't want to go in there, especially at night. I had to urinate so I slid down my pants and urinated at the foot of the cot. I was in distress. I didn't know how long they would keep me. I knew the people working there and the people staying there weren't right. They were everything I expected when the next morning came. We had breakfast. I don't think it was very good. I don't remember. After breakfast, mid morning the Doctor talked to me. He decided I could go. I got out the next day but one night is bad enough with those people. Andy picked me up and I pretended I was trying my best to get myself back together. I had been talking in a broken pattern for so long I did have a hard time talking normally.

He was sleeping with two or three other girls. He wasn't sleeping with me. We weren't making love anymore. He was doing pharmaceutical drugs one of my relatives smuggled in to him without my knowledge. He was trading the pills for the meth. I'm not an expert on meth. I do know they produced something that was sort of yellow in powder form.

One morning this girl showed up with ice, a stronger version of meth, in a plastic fold up envelope. This stuff was clear and had the consistency of plastic, soft plastic. You had to peel off a rectangle. The stuff made me sick at my stomach when I smelled it. I could smell it in her purse. She was getting it in Atlanta. Andy dropped it in the glass pipe and started smoking it. He smoked for three days and was progressively getting meaner and grouchier.

Belinda, a friend of mine, stopped by and told me I had no idea what Andy was doing. I didn't. He had morphine suckers, Oxycontin, and anything he wanted.

After Andy started beating on me and threatening to kill me I didn't hang out with him much. He always had somebody there. He always had porno on the television.

Andy was so bad off on drugs he didn't sleep. He had guys over all the time. He was threatening to kill me all the time. He would say "I'm going to kill you." I would use a loud tone of voice and say "Kill me. Kill me now. How long is it going to take and is it going to hurt?". These guys would trip over themselves they were leaving so fast. They were afraid of Andy and no one had ever talked to him like that. Finally I told him to quit threatening me and kill me. I wasn't afraid. I probably should have been.

About a month after I told him to quit threatening me and just kill me he put a gun in my mouth. I was in the restroom sitting on the toilet and he came in and put a gun in my mouth. I stared into his eyes and it seemed like forever. He never pulled the trigger. It seemed like it had been about five minutes. It was a long time to have a gun in your mouth. After he took the gun out of my mouth I went into the bedroom. Andy followed me and grabbed by the hair on the back of my head. He hit me twenty one times on the right side of my head with the gun. I know it was twenty one times because he counted every time he hit me. I didn't scream, or cry or respond in any way. This frustrated him and he stopped hitting me on the head with the gun and slung me across the room. I don't remember what I did after that.

Now I was in a terrible situation. I was living with a man that was supposedly a DEA Agent, definitely was a criminal and a felon and I had no one to help me.

The door of the master bedroom was heavy and Andy had said the room was bullet proof. That didn't stop him from shooting at me. He had a gun he said had a hair trigger. He shot at me four times in the bedroom. I had always told him he could shoot at me but God wouldn't let him shoot me. I was sure of that. He gave the gun to Jim the next time he came to the house and told him it had a hair trigger and laughed. I knew then he had been shooting at me.

One day Andy had a meeting with a "friend" that I wasn't privy to. They talked for about an hour. He drove a red pickup truck. Andy told me he paid him back a loan from years back. It was $3000 dollars. Andy told me we were going to Florida. It was funny because he handed me a one hundred dollar bill and told me to feel of it. I felt of it and didn't feel anything wrong but I didn't know it was counterfeit and that Andy had just purchased counterfeit money. I knew about the $3000. After all was said and done he told me he had more buried on the other side of the road where the barn was. I set about putting the house in order to leave for a week and go to Florida. He said not to take any clothes, we would buy new ones. I was looking forward to that. step was to cut the strip that you light the matches with off. It took a case to make enough phosphorus. All three of us were cutting match books. I don't know who fell asleep first. When I woke up all the matches hadn't been cut and Andy was hollering at me to get up and get in the truck. We left Terry in the house to clean up.

Andy had a gun and made me get in the truck. The gun was a sawed off shotgun. The shotgun was illegally sawed off. It was pretty though. It had mother of pearl inlays and was white. I had Terry witness this. He lived on Beer Can Road with his mother in a trailer. He was standing on the carport when Andy made me get in the truck. He stayed behind and cleaned up the house. He did a really good job.

After I got in the truck I ate a peanut butter sandwich and washed it down with water. I was waiting. As we pulled out of the driveway I took some Soma and went to sleep. Andy woke me up once to write a check at a convenience store somewhere. I wasn't fully awake but Andy said if I didn't give him a check the man was going to call the police.

While we were in jail the FBI or some Federal Law Enforcement went in the house. The first door they tried had a pane of glass missing just in the right place to put an arm in and unlock the door. Before we left I glued a clothes line clip to the counter inside. The Law Enforcement officer cut his arm. I meant for the person going inside and stealing to get cut and I would know who it was. I was tired of finding my stuff gone.

He had spent the night with us cutting matches. We all fell asleep. Andy and I were on the couch and he was in a rocking chair. I took some Soma and slept all day. He got charged for the counterfeit money in one county that I didn't know until I got out of jail. He woke me up once to write a check. He said he needed a check so I gave it to him rather than having it taken away from me. I just went along with him so he wouldn't hit me. We parked in his brother's driveway and slept for a little while. He was sleepy and ready to do drugs. We had just left a couple's house that kept two milligram Xanax and Chief had taken some. He never took one of anything. I had begged him to stop at a hotel. He went through the same fast food restaurant drive through again. The police were waiting. He saw them walking up and gave me some money to hold. When the police man got to the window he said give me that money. There I was. He got me arrested on purpose. That is love. I waited seven days and finally got out when some friends of his bonded their house. I didn't get away with my furniture, clothes, shoes, china, dishes, pans, art work, decorations, priceless pictures of my children, nothing. I got nothing back. The way I left was in a hurry. I put on old clothes, ran next door.

Everyone in my family came to my aide but they looked at me as if I was dangerous. I was in shock and couldn't talk about what I'd been through. My cousin took me in at my Daddy's bequest. He has a degree in Psychology so I guess they thought he could cure me and watch me for dangerous behavior, I painted a sign that said "The best thing in life is in doing what others say you can not." He took that wrong.

Chapter 31

I WAS SO stupid I was happy to see Chief when I saw him again. I jumped up in his arms and said now we'll have to get married so I can't testify against you. He got the diamonds he'd smuggled in from Columbia back from his mother the thief way and was going to have me a ring made from them.

He had smuggled these diamonds out of Columbia in the seams of his shirts and jeans. He got back and he was the diamond man. Then he got into trouble for writing prescriptions that he then decided to try to "cash". Medication means money to Chief. Since he was twelve his was selling a hit with your own sharp for twenty dollars and you could sit around his house and do dope. Mepregan, with a needle. He did it all the time and Quaaludes. He wrecked his car, flew off the road into the top of the trees and then he opened the door and fell down from the top of the trees. He told me so many things that he did that were mean I didn't know what to think about myself. I was so attracted to what was for all intents and purposes was a sick, master manipulator, psychopath.

I may have been diagnosed Bipolar after the fact but at least there was a logical reason why I would think that Chief would be good to me and love me. He told me so. I think he lies. Every time we broke up one of us made the first move and started seeing each other exclusively. If we were together we were together. It was wild. I couldn't understand why when he put that gun in my mouth I wasn't afraid because I could look in his eyes and see his love for me. What was he doing? Only God knows literally.

I needed my right hand ring re-shanked—2 carats. I was so stupid I put my ring in with his diamonds in his name. He was supposed to be having an engagement ring made for me. I haven't seen my ring since. I guess someone he knows is wearing it or he sold it. He also destroyed my gold nugget 18kt gold chain and nugget. It was heavy enough to clang against my teeth if I bent over wrong. I let him wear it and while I was hiding because he was going to kill me he cut gold off it and dunked it in gold paint. I couldn't even register this emotionally and still haven't actually. I'll be on probation quite a few more years. Its first offenders so I won't have a record, but this is so embarrassing. He got me arrested on purpose because he wanted to.

We were at a fast food restaurant, for the second time, when he saw the police walking up. He handed me some money and told me to put it in my pants. I did. Then the police were at the window. He told me to give him back the money. That was enough to get me arrested. I didn't know what for until Monday morning. We were arrested Saturday night at about 11:00 pm.

When we got out we went to stay with his alcoholic dad and step mom. We stayed there about a week. Andy was afraid to go back to the house. He was afraid the FBI was watching the house. Times there were tense. Andy kept going across the street to an old friend of his house and shooting up. His stepmother usually slept in the upstairs bedroom we slept in. His dad ended up pulling a gun on us and we left. I took the gun pretty serious since he had killed two people when Andy was five. Andy was watching. He wanted to cash my personal check. I had given him a check for $400.00 per month for "rent". He spent it and any other money I had for meth.

He was always pawning something to get money for meth. When he ran out of things to pawn he took me into the pawn shop. Right then and there he took two gold bracelets off my arm and made me pawn them. I never got them back. I was forced to sell my jewelry right then and there. I was robbed in essence.

Chapter 32

WHEN HIS DADDY showed us the door with a gun we rode around in his dad's car. I was so tired I got in back and went to sleep. When I woke up or rather he woke me up, I got back in the front seat. Andy went to my bank and wanted to cash the "rent" check. They wouldn't cash it at the drive through. Andy took it away from me and went inside and cashed it. He was hitting me on the side of the head and hurting me. I started to cry. I hadn't had one moments peace in fifteen days. I was exhausted.

He went to Jim and Jill's and I told them he was hitting me. They let me lay down in their daughters bed. They made Andy leave. Then Jill took me to a hotel and bought me some food. I ate a whole jar of peanut butter. I ate salads with grilled chicken in them. I ate anything I had and slept the whole time. They also gave me some money. Monday morning I walked next door to the restaurant and bought two pieces of chocolate pie. That was breakfast. They paid for me to check out Monday and told me to call someone to come and get me. I thought about it Sunday night and called my Uncle to come get me. He got there about 9:00 Monday morning.

I tried to tell him what I'd been through but he didn't believe me. He just didn't think something so absurd really happened. He also thought I was addicted to meth. I told him I wasn't. My Uncle drinks and had offered me two hundred and fifty dollars to get naked and let him touch me. He didn't bother me like that while I stayed with him for two days. The second day I called a friend, and she came and took me back to the mountain. Andy was there and they were cooking in the bedroom. The carpet caught on fire. They were trying to use the fireplace. I'm glad the fire went out with a bed spread covering it. I wanted all my things back. I wanted my children's Hallmark Christmas tree ornaments dating bake to 1980. I wanted my Great Grandfather's dresser circa 1890. I wanted my Great Grandmother's china and my Grandmothers china. I wanted everything that had been moved into the house and I thought being there was the best way to get out of there with my belongings.

Andy was happy to see me and told me that Jim had told him I never wanted to see him again. I was still unreasonably wrong in love but I knew he was never going to change.

I told my friend to never go back without me. She did anyway. She got busted with meth ingredients in her car. She had been going there or staying there about six weeks before she got arrested. I told her she would get arrested. I haven't talked to her since.

Larry was gone. Andy had made him leave. Before he left he cooked meth in the garage. He stayed about a week before he finally left. After he left I took the electric eyes off the stove so no one else could go in there and cook. There was still a microwave and they probably figured out how to cook with that.

I was with Andy on the mountain for about two more weeks. It was a Sunday morning when I left with the police and went to the mental hospital. I was just waking when Andy came in. He had a sharp in his hand. That's when he gave me the big shot. I had never felt anything like that. I was so afraid. Fear was my first reaction. I jumped up and put on clothes. I went to the neighbor's house. They were surprised to see me so shaken up. I was ok, I was just so anxious. I asked them to go to the bathroom thinking that their house might be wired for light and sound also. That made them nervous. They had always ignored Chief. He acted like he had good sense when he talked to them. He called the man the "Sheriff". I wish I had asked them if they had heard Andy threatening to kill me. I just didn't think about that, I was thinking about getting away alive. They had on their pajamas still it was so early. I asked them to call the police to pick me up from the bridge on the cross road.

I left their house from the back door. I heard Andy call my name. He had gone into the bathroom to shoot up. He was running out of veins. Sometimes, fairly often, I watched him try to shoot up for hours. The syringe would be all full of blood. If he couldn't get a vein and got tired of trying he would shoot the contents of the syringe across the room. I never said anything because he was the kind of person you didn't tell what to do or even act like you saw him. That was the nastiest thing I've ever seen anybody, in my whole life, do. His arms looked like he had been stuck in a briar patch. That is exactly what he told me the first time I saw him.

It seemed to take hours to get to the tall grass where the police were supposed to pick me up. There was a fence I couldn't get around so I had to get in the lake and swim to get to the other side. I slid into the water and swam to the other side. I pulled myself out of the lake. I was soaking wet. I was scared. I was thinking in terms of life or death. The police drove up just as I got the bushes to crouch down. I looked around me for snakes and found a mask. A black eye hole and mouth hole mask. I left it. I knew it was supposed to be there. It was evidence that someone had been there and watched for something. I think it was the people Andy had told me were watching the house.

Chapter 33

WHILE I WAS with my husband at his sister's house the friends of Andy's that had bonded me out of jail with a property bond called me very frequently. They had my cousin's phone line bugged. I talked to Penny every day. They were keeping a close eye on me. My Daddy contacted them and I don't know what he said but they took my bond away. Penny was always saying how much my Daddy loved me. She said my Daddy would get me out. My Daddy did not get me out. My mother told him not to. There was no place for me to go.

Penny called me one day and said my Daddy had rented me a partially furnished apartment. I didn't call my Daddy to verify this story. Penny told me Alan was coming to get me. Alan took me to jail and they went off my property bond. I spent the next fifty eight days in jail.

Jail is not like it is on movies. I was in a cell with a schizophrenic woman. She played solitaire and talked to people who weren't there. I ignored her or was nice to her, depending on what she was doing. Some people thought I was addled brained to be put in a cell with her. The doors on our cell didn't close. We were on the honor system to stay inside our cell. She was always pulling the Velcro on her shoes at night. She didn't sleep. I just ignored her. I could sleep through just about everything.

Then we got a new cell mate. She had just come from State Prison and had a hold on her that got her in county jail. She provoked my cellmate until there was a fight. I got knocked back onto the toilet and hurt my back. Thelma Lou, my cellmate, got two weeks in solitaire. I felt sorry for her.

While I was in jail I couldn't take my medication for Bipolar. I couldn't take any of my medications. My husband did bring me Geodon one time. He also sent me money so that on Fridays when they had "store" I could buy candy, envelopes, long johns, etc. It was high to get things from the store. They sold the conditioner, lotion, etc. that said on the bottle "Donated by Bob Barker". I never had enough money to get long johns. That's what I needed. I thought I was going to freeze to death in jail. I had to put my one blanket over my head so my breath would warm me up.

We were searched one morning at 2:00 am for a cell check. Someone was smoking cigarettes they got to the back somehow. We all had to go out into the hall and sit on the floor. They took us one by one and searched us after they searched the cells and didn't find anything.

The food in jail was terrible. There was never anything like salad or anything that didn't come out of a can or a box I was told was marked "Not for Human Consumption". I craved salad. I craved anything but what we were being fed. Chili came with rice. Everything came with rice so it would be cheaper and I guess more filling. For lunch we got two cookies and for dinner we got a piece of cake. No icing, just cake. I thought that was nice. At least they let you have something sweet. You got a luke warm glass of some fruit flavored drink that was about five ounces to drink. The rest of the time you had to drink from the fountain on the back of the toilet.

Going to the toilet was an experience. Everything you did someone or lots of someone's could watch you. They didn't as far as I know, but

I ignored the fact that forty or so women and some men guards could watch me go the restroom.

In jail I got one two inch thick mat for the steal bunk, one top sheet and one bottom sheet. I got one blanket. I made myself a pillow out of menstrual pads and it helped my neck. It was confiscated during a Sunday night inspection. I got two orange outfits for the week. I got one roll of toilet paper, one bottle of shampoo, one bar of soap. I had to take off my bra, panties and socks to rinse them out in the sink. I had to hang then from a torn off piece of sheet to dry. While they were drying I had none to wear.

Sometimes you got the orange suit without writing, sometimes you got the orange suit that had everything under the sun written on them with a pencil. Pencils you had to buy. They were about four inches long. You had to buy paper and postage. I was writing to my husband. He was the only person that was checking on me. That I could call. He wrote me bible verses sometimes and sometimes he just wrote. He had one of his old friends from the southern part of the state send me a card. I was so embarrassed.

After fifty eight days the first thing I did was give them back the things that weren't disposable and throw away things I'd been wearing in jail.

Being out of jail was wonderful. I realized my husband was a very good man and I went back to his sister's house where he was living. We lived there seven months and got our own apartment. I am thankful I have my husband. He is so good to me. I will do anything for him. I love really love him and couldn't face life without him.

After fifty eight days I had enough money to pay my bond. It was one thousand dollars. My husband came on a Friday night with a bondsman and I was finally out of jail. I spent the whole summer locked up somewhere.

The last time I saw Randy was in Court. He had missed Court two times and I was told charges against me would be dropped. He was there with the City Attorney the last time. He got twenty five years of probation for having liquid meth, a needle, an illegally sawed off shotgun that didn't belong to him, counterfeit money. He was already a Felon and he should have gone to jail. I'll never know why he didn't. His Attorney told the Judge he was attending college to get a degree for rehabilitating people with alcohol and drug problems. He had been educated in getting people to use drugs. I don't know how he got out of going to jail. His Uncle is the head of the State Probation program. I'm sure that had something to do with his not going to jail. I got seven years probation and a fine. I didn't have a record. I had one DWI from seven years before but that was all. I learned my lesson and took cabs if I wanted to go out.

I've never cried about all that I lost. I'm afraid if I start I'll never stop. They must have destroyed my children's newborn baby pictures. I did get back some pictures, but not all of them. Randy probably burned them.

Chapter 34

WHILE STAYING WITH my cousin I had a Psychiatrist appointment. My Uncle had his live in slave, basically, to take me to the appointment. I tried to get my ring back but the man that owned the jewelry store wouldn't give it to me. I paid the psychiatrist three hundred and seventy dollars. The budget my cousin planned for me was blown for the month. I decided to pick up some clothes I needed. I had lost everything.

I was waiting on my cousin to pick me up and take me back with him. He delayed it for two days. One Friday night he was supposed to be coming to get me. There was a knock at the door and I thought it was my cousin. When I opened the door it was my husband.

The first thing he said was "You are still my wife." I said I know and stepped out on the porch to talk to him. He wanted me to leave my Uncle's and go with him to his sister's house. I knew my cousin was nervous and afraid of what I might do so I went with my husband. He took me to his sister's house. Then he took me to the bar where we met. I still wanted to go to Shane's house. My husband was taking me there but it was dark and I didn't know how to get back. I called once and didn't understand the directions.

I had accumulated enough that I needed a suitcase. I bought a suitcase and a day timer. I need a day timer to know what and when I'm supposed to be and what I will be doing.

We refer to these two years as a vacation. We are still together and since I've been taking medication for Bipolar. I am doing great. I'm happy with my life. I'm thankful I'm still alive.

The key to managing Bipolar is to take your medication every day like clockwork. I keep my medication in a seven day organizer and once a week I go through and fill the organizer up. Then all I have to do is get one day's worth of medication and take it in the morning, at noon or one o'clock., at five or six and at bedtime. Sometimes I can't sleep at night and I stay up all night. I used to be a night owl but now I can go to bed anytime. I get up eight hours later no matter what. Sometimes I get woke up and can't go back to sleep.

I see my doctor monthly. I don't know yet how I feel about revealing these two years of my life. I just think my story is worth telling. The stuff in this book happened to me. I wasn't in a movie, even if it did seem like it sometimes. Most of the time. Ninety nine percent of the time. After all, there were lights, camera, action. Chief asked me if I could see the cameras one time. I think he was telling me where they were located. I guess he wanted me to go "off" camera to do some things. At least I hope something we had was private. Knowing Chief I'm holding out hope in the wrong thing.

I do thank God that I lived through this. Sometimes God must send in a warrior. That is how I see this experience. I was sent to do battle and I was removed before I got in too much danger. God has to have warriors to reach some people. In just the short time I was there I know one soul went to heaven. A man that was an atheist asked me about God and Jesus. He listened intensely to what I had to say. He thanked me and he left with some other people he had come with. I never saw him again. He died the next week.